"Rejoice in the Lord alway: and again I say, Rejoice!"
(Philippians 4:4)

Marlene Evans

Other Books by Marlene Evans

Pattern for Living

Pattern for Living Teacher's Manual

Cancer: My Enemy, My Friend

There's Life After Cancer

Help Lord! They Call Me Mom

Comfort for Hurting Hearts

*Christian Womanhood Cookbook
and Homemaker's Guide*

I'm Going to Live Until I Die

New Hope: Be the Parent You Were Meant to Be

Redbirds and Rubies and Rainbows

*A Daily Chat with Marlene Evans
Around the Bible*

The Life Series
Marriage Without Divorce
Relationships Without Regrets
Kids Without Chaos
Sickness Without Despair
Teens Without Turmoil

The Five Sins of Christian Women

by
Dr. Marlene Evans

copyright © 2002
Christian Womanhood
8400 Burr Street
Crown Point, Indiana 46307
219-365-3202
e-mail: chrwoman@netnitco.net

ISBN: 0-9719019-4-5

Scriptures used in this book are excerpts
from the King James Bible.

Cover Design:
BerylMartin

Printed and Bound in the United States of America
Dickinson Press Inc., Grand Rapids, MI

Dedication

In loving memory
of
our mentor, boss, and friend

Marlene Evans

About the Author

MARLENE EVANS AUTHORED 17 books. Mrs. Evans earned a Bachelor of Science degree in secondary education and a Master of Arts degree in Christian education from Bob Jones University, a Master of Education degree in Educational Organization and Supervision from the University of Tennessee, and a Doctor of Humanities degree from Hyles-Anderson College. She was recognized in the list of "Who's Who Among Teachers in America's Universities and Colleges." Mrs. Evans served as Dean of Women at Hyles-Anderson College for over 20 years and as a faculty member from 1972, the year the college opened, until her death in 2001. She taught speech, psychology courses, education courses, and Christian Womanhood, a unique course for Christian ladies.

In 1975, Mrs. Evans founded and began editing *Christian Womanhood*, a newspaper designed especially for fundamental Christian ladies. She also had to her credit over 100 speaking tapes on numerous subjects pertinent to today's women. Mrs. Evans' speaking and writing caused her to be a much sought-after conference speaker and led to the founding of the annual Christian Womanhood Spectacular, a ladies' conference at First Baptist Church of Hammond, Indiana, with a record attendance of over 7,000.

Her down-to-earth teaching and homespun humor were used of God to help ladies in their marriages, in their child rearing, in their service to God, and in all other relationships of life.

Acknowledgments

Thank you to Dan Wolfe who had the vision and the wisdom to see the great value of putting Mrs. Evans' classic into book form.

Thank you to Linda Stubblefield for editing, compiling, and preparing the manuscript for press.

Thank you to Mrs. Cindy Schaap and Mrs. Jane Grafton who read the book for continuity and clarity and made sound editorial suggestions.

Thank you to Mrs. Cathy Kimmel who typed the preliminary manuscript and the doses of Scripture Bible verses for this book.

Thank you to Miss Bethany Stubblefield for spending her mornings transcribing tapes to help with this project.

Thank you to Rena Fish, with whom we have worked for many years with the proofreading, who continues to proofread with excellence.

Thank you to Brother and Mrs. Jack Schaap who saw the continued need for the ministry of *Christian Womanhood*. Without their blessing and support, this book would not have been published.

"MARLENE EVANS WAS one of the greatest Christians I have ever known. She gave herself completely to others— day and night." —*Mrs. Caroline Roberson*
wife of Dr. Lee Roberson
founder of Tennessee Temple University

"HAVING WORKED WITH women and girls many years, Mrs. Evans really knew women and how they 'ticked.' She had a God-given burden to help us to see through the mirror of her wisdom how we need to change and thereby how we can go a long way in changing the dangerous trend our country is taking. Thank you, Marlene Evans."
— *Mrs. Beverly Hyles*
wife of Dr. Jack Hyles
founder of Hyles-Anderson College

"BY HER YEARS of successful service to multitudes and her proven literary ability, Dr. Marlene Evans endeared herself to a wide constituency, all of whom will readily grab at the opportunity to read anything new from her pen.

She wrote the way she spoke—with excitement and lots of action! You who had not the pleasure of knowing her personally will quickly get the feeling she is no longer a stranger as you enjoy her sense of humor, marvel at her kaleidoscopic career, and above all, sense her Christian love and concern, not only for those at her home base, but for women and girls all over America." — *Dr. Viola Walden*
assistant to Dr. John R. Rice

Table of Contents

Foreword by Mrs. Cindy Schaap ~ 11
Introduction by Mrs. Marlene Evans ~ 15

Part I — The Prevention of the Five Sins ~19

Part II — The Diagnosis of the Five Sins ~ 43
    Chapter 1—Nerves, Worry, and Depression / 45
    Chapter 2—Gossip and a Critical Spirit / 57
    Chapter 3—Lack of Loving Your Husband and Children / 77
    Chapter 4—Immodest Dress / 97
    Chapter 5—Lack of Soul Winning, Bible, and Prayer / 117

Part III — The Antidote for the Five Sins ~143

Part IV — The Sixth Sin of Christian Women ~161
    Chapter 1—Jealousy / 163
    Chapter 2—Can I Be First? / 171

Part V — Conclusion ~179

Part VI — Doses of Scripture ~ 185

A Note from the Publishers by Dan Wolfe ~255

Foreword
by Mrs. Cindy Schaap

I was privileged to read the manuscript of *The Five Sins of Christian Women* before it was sent out for publication. I enjoyed reading it very much. I found it helpful to have a narrowed-down list of those things on which Christian women most typically need to work. I discovered the antidotes and the emphasis on Scripture to be both practical and spiritually beneficial.

All of the book was formulated through Mrs. Evans' live speaking tapes. Though I found the book to be very readable, there were parts of the book which skipped around a bit sporadically as a live speaker might be prone to do. Some of these areas I changed, and some I left the same. I wanted to make the book as readable as possible **without** removing the personality of Marlene Evans. Please bear with Christian Womanhood if, in places, the book is less than easy to follow. Picture in your mind a live speaker giving these truths to an audience with whom she always seems to feel at home. With that picture in mind, you will better enjoy your reading. I, for one, thoroughly enjoyed seeing Mrs. Evans' personality in this book. I felt for a brief time that the personality of a woman I loved and admired had come down from Heaven to earth for a wonderfully helpful visit.

I finished reading the manuscript on a summer Friday evening. I was sitting on my front porch waiting for my husband to arrive home from work when a paragraph from the end of the book grabbed my attention and convicted my soul.

"Oh, my dream and my burden for the girls at Hyles-Anderson College is that they be different. It is my dream that every man who is married to a Hyles-Anderson College girl will have a jewel—one of God's precious gems. She might not be beautiful, and perhaps won't be smart. There may be things she is not, but if she loves her husband, if she dresses modestly, if she wins souls, if she does not have a critical spirit, if she doesn't have a gossiping tongue, if she doesn't run around all nervous, worried, and depressed, that man has a JEWEL!"

So many times I have heard people say that the students at Hyles-Anderson College are different. Their loving spirits are the first thing that you notice about them. That is in great part, I'm sure, due to the ministry and the dream of our first Dean of Women, Marlene Evans.

I now work as the Senior Editor of *Christian Womanhood*, a ministry that Marlene Evans founded, with her coworkers whom she influenced. I notice in them that same loving spirit. It is so rare for a woman who works with Christian Womanhood to say something hurtful to someone, that if the slightest mistreatment occurs, we are almost taken aback with shock.

That is not to say that these ladies are perfect, but rarely is my time with them anything but stress-free and pleasant. I have seen the circumstances surrounding them become stressful, but when the flesh nature shows up, they seem to be well trained on how to control their own spirits and how to apologize when mistakes occur.

As I have read this manuscript, I have realized that Marlene Evans' dream has come true. She managed to reproduce herself and to influence a generation of ladies for God and for right. Tears of rejoicing came to my eyes as I thought of the fruition of Mrs. Evans' noble dream.

Seconds later, however, my heart was filled with conviction. I realized that, as the pastor's wife of First Baptist Church of Hammond, the Chancellor's wife Hyles-Anderson College, and the Senior Editor of *Christian Womanhood*, it is largely up to women like myself to see that her dream continues on—to see that the upcoming generation of ladies learn the great, Bible-based way of life that was Mrs. Evans' dream.

I am reminded that it is not position that makes a woman successful; it is the influence of her spirit to those around her. In the truest respect, Marlene Evans was successful in her life on earth.

Each day I ask God to give me a portion of Marlene Evans' spirit. It is not that I am trying to be like her, nor am I trying to take her place. But, as a leader in *Christian Womanhood*, I feel like I owe it to Marlene Evans and to her loved ones to carry on the spirit of the "different woman" to the next generation.

I highly commend the life of the author of this book. I highly recommend the truths of the material found in this book. I highly recommend the product of those truths. I urge you to read this book, to learn the spirit of its truth, and to be a part of carrying Mrs. Evans' dream and the spirit of Christ to the next generation of ladies.

Introduction
by Marlene Evans

IN MARCH 1975, Dr. Hyles asked me to speak on the subject of "Christian Womanhood" for the ladies who were to attend Pastors' School. Many ladies helped me present material on how to win souls, how to teach girls to be ladies, how to be submissive to husbands, and how to organize your time in order to be a keeper at home and a church worker—both for the glory of God.

I also teach a course at Hyles-Anderson College called "Christian Womanhood." Pat Hays, a woman who had just moved to the Hammond area to put her three children into Hammond Baptist Schools, took a few of my courses that year. She had sent me notes asking questions regarding my publishing the materials I was giving in class. I said, "Mrs. Hays, I can't even write a letter. I surely cannot write a book."

She did private duty nursing at night once in a while, and one day I received a $17.35 check in my mail from some nursing agency with the message: "This is to go to help you put some of your teaching on tape." Well, since I wasn't planning anything such as that, I ignored the whole thing. (I did keep the money though!)

When Pat heard that I was to speak at Pastors' School, she asked me if she could drive me to the church every day so I would not have to think about being late, parking, or anything that could possibly hinder my being with the ladies. Then she asked if I were going to make some tapes since there are usually facilities for selling them at conferences.

Finally, I agreed to make *a* tape about "The Five Sins of Christian Women" which included my main emphases: nerves, worry, and depression; gossip and a critical spirit; lack of soul winning, Bible, and prayer; lack of love for husband and children; and immodest dress. After I made one 60-minute tape, I found I wasn't finished. I made another and still wasn't through, so I just concluded with the third one. I did not have time to organize the making of those tapes; it was Pastors' School time when I agreed to make them. I said the same things on several of them, and I have personally never heard such terrible "yakking" as I heard when I received the test tapes. (Several thousands of sets later, they are still the same yakking.)

"Who will buy my tapes?" I asked. "No one will want to buy a set of those and pay $9.00 for them. Order only 25 sets; nobody will want that junk." When Pat asked if we couldn't get at least 100 sets, I finally said, "Okay, but I surely hate to have them sitting around cluttering up the place."

Preachers would pass by the sales table and ask about the tapes. Pat would name off the five points and then say, "If you buy these tapes and don't like them, I want you to bring them back. You see, only certain people are to have these. If you have a tape recorder with you, listen to one side and be sure they are what you want. Do you understand? These tapes are to be listened to and used. They will change the lives of the ladies in your church. If you are going to put them up on on a shelf, please don't buy them."

I have no doubt some were thinking, "That's not the way to sell!" Maybe it isn't, but by the time I returned for the evening session, all 100 sets of "The Five Sins of Christian Women" had been sold! I couldn't believe my eyes, but the money Pat handed to me was proof. I allowed her to order another 100 sets. The second evening session came, and I checked on how many sets were left. Once again I was shown an empty table. (I was relieved to be out of debt!)

I spoke to three groups of ladies every day. We ordered 300 total sets that week. I knew women were whiney, gossipy, com-

INTRODUCTION

plaining, nervous individuals, but I did not know how much they did not want to be until that week in March, 1975.

At the closing session of Pastors' School, Brother Hyles had a parade of workers. As we paraded up into the choir loft and looked out into the great audience of people, I started crying uncontrollably. Pat did not cry at all, but she watched me and the women in the audience. They had been asking, "Will you come to our church to speak to our ladies?"

I had had to say, "No" because I carefully limit my speaking engagements because of my family and my work.

I was asked, "Is there a book that would help us to know how to help girls become interested in being ladies?"

Again, I had to say, "No."

They even asked, "If the girls want to be ladies, how do you teach them?" One commented, "I live on the coast of Oregon, and everyone would think I was crazy if I wore a skirt. Can someone write to me once in a while to encourage me?"

A lady from Canada said, "I haven't stopped crying since I got here. I didn't know there could be love among Christian women like this! I don't want to go home."

One young, pretty wife explained, "I didn't want to come here with my husband. He made me come, but I told myself I would not listen to a thing you said. Now I want to hear a lot more, and I can't."

The emotional strain and excitement of the week, plus the cries of those ladies were the reason for my sobs. Needless to say, I was emotionally drained when I reached home that Friday and was trying to get ready to turn right around to go to Logansport, Indiana, where my husband was preaching that weekend.

I was getting the kids' things ready, feeling as if I had been chewed up and spit out, when Pat called with, "What are you going to do about it?"

"About what?" I asked.

"Well, you're not just going to give them what you told them at Pastors' School and then just leave them, are you?"

"Yep, I sure am, and I've gotta go to Logansport."

That night, the next day, and Sunday I thought of those women. For some reason, I kept thinking particularly of the one on the Oregon coast—she felt so alone. When I returned home on Monday, I told Pat we were starting a ministry if our preacher okayed it. He did, and we were off and running!

PART ONE

*The Prevention
of the Five Sins of Christian Women*

The Prevention
of the Five Sins of Christian Women

WHEN I FIRST began speaking to groups of ladies or girls, I would give Philippians 4:4 and talk about what I called the five sins of Christian women. When I was 28 years of age, the great teaching of Philippians 4:4 was made real to me by my Sunday school teacher. This teacher, Mrs. Louise Holbrook, came into my life and said, "Marlene, if you live long enough, you are going to have problems. That's the way of life."

As I understood "problems," I hadn't had any problems. I had a good home with parents who loved me. I had not known any health problems. I couldn't remember being sick. I had my tonsils taken out—you know, the general, ordinary things—but as far as being sick, I had had no problems. I had not even been through childbirth, for our children are adopted.

Of course, when you are growing up, you **think** you have problems. I had the usual, ordinary problems such as not being popular, but no *real* problems. Tragedy had not come into my life. Two grandfathers and a grandmother whom I loved had died, but that's about the most serious heartache I had experienced.

However, Mrs. Holbrook had reminded me more than once that if I lived long enough, I would have problems. Her verse was, *"Rejoice in the Lord alway: and again I say, Rejoice."* She loved the whole Bible, but that verse was the one that particularly helped her.

Therefore, she often said, "Marlene, I am not asking you to rejoice in your troubles; I am not asking you to rejoice in the sickness you might have some day. I am not asking you to rejoice when perhaps a child is killed or a child dies in your home. I am not asking you to rejoice in that kind of situation. I am asking you to rejoice in the LORD!"

Philippians 4:4 says, *"Rejoice in the Lord alway: and again I say, Rejoice."* With the understood subject, "YOU," rejoicing is a command; it is not just a suggestion. The Word of God says, "YOU" rejoice in the Lord always, not just when there are good times, and not just when there are bad times. There are some people who can really stand up under pressure and look stronger than when they have no pressure. You have known those types of people who seem to thrive on problems and troubles and are just great during such a time. This verse, however, says, **always** rejoice in the Lord.

Mrs. Holbrook called me on the telephone every day and sometimes talked an hour. In the course of our conversations, sooner or later I would start griping and complaining: "I don't like that Sunday school class!" "I don't like so-and-so!" "I don't like what so-and-so does."

She would respond with, "Honey! Oh, honey!"

Mentally I would retort, "Oh, Honey, nothing! You don't see what those women do!"

Then she would add, "But we just don't gripe! We just don't complain! No!"

And I'd say, "I do!"

As she drilled and drilled away and talked to me, she quoted another verse: *"In every thing give thanks: for this is the will of God in Christ Jesus concerning you."* (I Thessalonians 5:18)

Finally, I'm glad to say, the teaching began to come through. Now it is my goal to live the kind of life that, no matter what happens to me, I rejoice in the Lord always.

I cannot tell you that I might not fall before your eyes tomorrow. All I know is, this verse is TRUE! It is the Word of God, and we can make it true in our lives, that is, as much as we will let the Holy Spirit work through us.

The Prevention

God Knows We Can't Rejoice in Our Troubles!

Philippians 4:4-8 is the Scripture I want you to read and study. God is so great! One reason why is that He knows we can't rejoice in our troubles. He understands we are not going to rejoice and clap our hands and say, "Goody, goody, goody, my baby is sick!" He didn't ask us to do that. God is a sensible God. He didn't ask us to do any such thing. He doesn't ask us to say, "Our money is almost gone; we're in school; my husband lost his job. Good. I'm so glad that happened." Of course not!

He says, *"Rejoice in the **Lord** alway,"* and not rejoice in either good or bad. If you are rejoicing in your children above the Lord and if they are taken from you, of course, your rejoicing is gone. If you are rejoicing in money above the Lord, and if your money is taken from you, of course, your rejoicing is gone. No matter what you are rejoicing in, if you are rejoicing in anything above that of the Lord Jesus Christ, then your rejoicing is gone when that thing is gone. When you are rejoicing in the **Lord**, when you are just thanking Him and blessing Him for everything, it really will not matter what happens in your life.

A lady I met, while my husband was pastoring in North Carolina, Nancy Perry, lost her husband and then her home. Still, I watched her go forward as if nothing had happened. Then she lost her health. She had rheumatoid arthritis, and then the doctors said that she would spend many of her years in a wheelchair. She did, and she lived exactly what I'm trying to teach in this introduction. You will see it all around you if you consciously begin to look.

The Sunday school teacher who started to teach me this truth said, "Marlene, I have had all kinds of heartaches; yet, my life has been so good." Her name was Louise Renaker Holbrook. She married again on her seventieth birthday, but she had been widowed for fourteen years. She had lost her beloved husband David, the one who meant so much to her. Just the way she said, "David," you knew he was her *beloved* husband. After his death, she lived alone, but she said, "I'm never alone! I'm never alone because the Lord Jesus is always with me."

We, who were in her Sunday school class, called ourselves "girls." She called us "girls," but most of us were in our twenties at that time. We were still her "girls" even though she was 75 years old. We all loved it when she married Mr. Olin Holbrook. We could see that she truly lived, "Rejoice in the Lord alway: and again I say, Rejoice."

Philippians 4:5–7 says, *"Let your moderation be known unto all men. The Lord is at hand. Be careful for nothing; but in every thing by prayer and supplication with thanksgiving let your requests be made known unto God. And the peace of God, which passeth all understanding, shall keep your hearts and minds through Christ Jesus."* How can you be anxious for nothing or be careful for nothing? Never worry! Pray about everything. Worry about nothing! How do you do that? "By prayer and supplication with thanksgiving." That little phrase, "**with thanksgiving**," is the way you do it. "Thank You, Lord. Thank You, Lord. Thank You, Lord. Thank You that I'm sick, that You've allowed me to be sick and to have this hospital treatment that I'm having." "Thank You, Lord that when my child died that You've given me such comfort. You've given me the dying grace I have to have when a loved one dies. Thank You, Lord. Thank You, Lord. Thank You!" No matter what happens, "Thank You!" THEN…we are able to *"be careful for nothing; but in every thing by prayer and supplication with thanksgiving let your requests be made known unto God. And the peace of God, which passeth all understanding shall keep your hearts and minds through Christ Jesus."*

People who live this wonderful philosophy are an utter

The Prevention

amazement to the world. Now let me explain something. **"Trouble comes to the saved and the unsaved."** It comes to those who know Jesus and to those who do not know Him. The Bible says that the rain falls on the just and the unjust. *"...for he maketh his sun to rise on the evil and on the good, and sendeth rain on the just and on the unjust."* (Matthew 5:45)

If this life were just a deal where we could live for God and He would erase our troubles, then it would be the same thing as when the Devil said, "Oh, yes, if You would turn Your people over to me, they wouldn't live like this." We see in the story of Job that God told the Devil that He would deliver Job over for testing. God knew He could trust Job to be tried. *"But he knoweth the way that I take: when he hath tried me, I shall come forth as gold."* (Job 23:10)

I wonder if God can trust us like He trusted Job. This is not a deal where we make a bargain when we say, "Lord, I'll live for You," and He makes everything easy for us. I've heard women say, "She must just be living right. That person must be living right because she has no troubles."

Are you saying that the people who have troubles are living wrong, more so than the people who are not having outward troubles? We cannot go by this at all! God allows trouble, trials, and disappointments; He allows us to have them for many, many different reasons. We can look back and say, "Thank You, Lord Jesus. Thank You for letting me go through a hard place. I can understand a little bit more so that I can comfort others, and so I can glorify Jesus through the way in which I react to this trouble."

Trouble Comes to the Saved and to the Unsaved, but the Way You React to that Trouble Will Gain the Attention of the Whole World!

Now everyone should be able to rejoice when things are going well, but can you rejoice when you fail a test? Ladies, when you are home, you are taking tests—not like a school test, of course. When you fail some kind of a test that you are having in your home, can you still rejoice? If you can, you are a different woman; you are a different girl; you stand out; you are above the ordinary! In fact, you are extraordinary, and you are the kind to whom the world can point and say, "How do you do it? No matter what the tragedy in your life is and no matter what the problem, you seem always to be rejoicing! How in the world do you do it?"

You can say (as you point within you or toward Heaven), "I do not do it. The One within me is the One Who does it. The Holy Spirit lives through me; the Lord Jesus came and left the Holy Spirit to help me through these times." Now if you don't have Anyone within you, you are not a Christian. If you are not saved, then you have every reason in the world to go around all upset.

"When in Trouble, When in Doubt, Run in Circles, Scream and Shout!!"

That is the motto by which so many women live! I believe too many women and girls have that expression for their life's verse, and it is not from Scripture nor is it based on Scripture! We have all heard their frantic statements: like, "Oh! I don't know what I'm going to do; I feel like I'm going to pieces." When you plan a nervous breakdown, you have one! You are going to have one, and that is all there is to it! You are not going to be cheated out of it!! Women just expect women to go to pieces, throw their hands in the air, and declare, "I don't know what I'm going to do!" We expect it! No one is going to come to us for help if we just run about, screaming and shouting and having fits. No one is going to come to us when we are like the women of the world, having nervous breakdowns, much worry, and depression.

Ladies, we are not expecting that from YOU! We are

expecting you to be someone different, one who stands out from the ordinary! To be a "great" woman is not what we want; we want someone who can go through any tragedy or any problem. I just hope that someday you can say, "I did it!" Of course, I would not want you to have to suffer a tragedy, but there will undoubtedly be some. When you face some problem, and there has been a problem such as the death of a child, I hope that you will have learned how to suffer well, that you have been in the Word of God till you manifested Christ completely through that time.

"If You Live Long Enough, You Will Have Problems!"

My Sunday school teacher said, "Marlene, you will have to get ready. If you live long enough, you will have problems! They are going to come. Get ready! You have gone through nothing. You do not know how you will react. If you gripe and complain and whine and bicker over little things— over things that are of no consequence in your life whatsoever—what will you do when the big things come?"

It happened that something did come into my life. I certainly haven't suffered like many have, but the Lord has allowed me to do some suffering since the time Mrs. Holbrook started teaching me. I am sure He had her there to start preparing me.

My problem started when I could not turn my neck. I thought I had a simple crick. I thought, "Well, I've got one of those things in my neck, and in a few days it will be all right." For a couple of weeks, I turned stiff-necked. Then the problem went down into my collar bone and down into my shoulder, and soon my arm was numb. I remember teaching small children at the time, and I should have been out running and doing active things with them, but I wanted to just stay inside and hold my arm which was weak and numb, and it tingled.

Someone said, "I'll tell you what it is; it is one of those "itis" brothers, 'Burs' or 'Arthur' or one of those guys."

I thought, "Arthritis? I'm too young!" However, no one is too young for that, are they? I wasn't that young anyway.

I made a doctor's appointment. My neck was x-rayed. Finally, I was told, "There are just no discs. Little cushions called discs are usually between those sharp vertebrae that you feel in the back of your neck, and there are no discs in your neck! Yours are worn out completely."

Their x-rays and examinations revealed that my vertebrae were fusing together, pinching the nerve, causing numbness in my arm and a tingly sensation. The doctors said, "Go on this medicine for a while, and let's see if we can treat it without operating."

I said, "That's fine; that's good!!"

The doctors diagnosed my condition as "degenerative disc disease." I'd never heard of such a thing, but I learned that a little "cushion" between vertebrae is pretty important. The doctors had no idea what caused the disintegration, especially in my neck. To my knowledge, I had never had an injury there.

In other words, I was too young to have a 75-year-old spine. The doctor explained to me that our bodies usually build until age 21, and then they start degenerating. The human body starts into a natural downward trend at age 21. (Isn't it great that, as our body starts deteriorating and degenerating, the spirit can go higher and higher? The soul can be more and more beautiful! In other words, you can be young at heart!) This is not something about which to be sad. Just realize that God is over all and takes care of all these things and that you have His perfect will in your life.

I took the medicine for about nine months, but the problem worsened until the doctor finally said there would have to be an operation. He said, "Here is what we do. We take a piece of hip bone. We open the front of the neck, pull aside the

THE PREVENTION

vocal cords, and put the hip bone (ground into a fine powder) into the neck bone." I immediately thought of that song, "The hip bone connected to the neck bone...." As a matter of fact, I thought of all kinds of things!

I thought I would be afraid, but I can never remember being fearful during that time before the operation. I cannot describe the peace I had. Mrs. Holbrook, my Sunday school teacher, had helped me so much. Since I had learned, *"Rejoice in the Lord alway: and again I say, Rejoice!"* I was able to live that verse. I cannot remember having a fear—not for a minute!

I do remember calling Mom and Dad and saying, "You know, I don't know when I'm going to be afraid." I was planning on it. I guess I felt cheated that I was not afraid, but that is not to my credit. It is because someone had begun teaching me that I am in God's hands, and whatever He allows is perfectly all right!

The night before my surgery I was asked to sign a responsibility release paper in case my voice were completely ruined! I was told that I would have to be careful about physical work and that I was risking my voice. (I am a teacher!!) Yet, it didn't seem to phase me at all, and now all I can do is marvel.

"I Had a Wonderful, Beautiful Operation!"

To make a long story short, I had two operations. When the doctors removed the piece of my hipbone, I thought, "Wow! I'll be smaller!" (But they only took a little bit.) When I woke up, my arm wasn't numb anymore. It was great! Mine was a wonderful, beautiful operation! I felt better right away—better than I had felt for months and months and months.

To those of you who have had so much more in your life or will have so much more in your life, remember that He will help you the same way He helped me through that time. There will be nothing to fear once you get it into your mind,

"Rejoice in the LORD always," so you can say, "Praise the Lord! Thank You, Lord, for letting me go through this. Thank You for the good hospital you've given me. Thank You for the friends—especially those who take care of my children. Thank You for a husband who stands by me." I had so many things for which to be thankful that I never did remember when to be afraid. How I thank God that a woman started talking to me and telling me, "*Rejoice in the LORD alway: and again I say, Rejoice!*"

How We Need to Help One Another!

How I thank God that a woman took the time to teach me! **A woman!** Could you be that woman in someone's life? How we desperately need women to help girls, older women to help middle-aged women! How we need to help one another!

The late Mrs. John R. Rice once said to me, "Marlene, there just aren't enough women to speak. Some who have so much to offer and live good lives, say, 'No, I couldn't talk to women!' " Mrs. Rice was already speaking to women; yet, she said there needed to be more who would speak to women.

Could you talk to women? Ask God to give you a burden that will overcome any fear that you might have. Oh, I don't mean that you won't be afraid, but whatever He wants you to do, "*Rejoice in the Lord alway; and again I say, Rejoice!*" I plead with some of you ladies who will be reading this book to ask God what He would have you to do. We need some ladies and some girls who will accept a burden to help others. Many times, girls will listen to a preacher and then say, "Oh, he doesn't know about wearing short skirts and not going along with the crowd as far as clothes are concerned. He doesn't understand."

But when a woman says, "This is the way it is, this is the way it should be, and it can be this way," those same girls have to listen because they know that she has gone through the same thing.

Could you ask God to help you to teach, whether it is indi-

The Prevention

vidually, one on one, or whether it is living a Christlike life for girls to emulate? Ladies, could you ask God to make you that which you should be so that young girls will have someone whom they can respect? Sometimes girls have to look only to men. I'm so glad they can look to the great men of God, and we want to put up those men before them. Always put up the man of God before the girls as someone for whom to pray, as someone to listen to, as someone to follow, as someone for whom to praise God; BUT, to what women are we pointing them?

Ladies, who are you? What could you do that would enable you to be someone to whom girls could look? I am so afraid that the women's lib movement has some basis for truth, and I hate the movement. I believe, if we Christian women had been what we should have been and if we had given young girls someone to whom to look, perhaps that movement wouldn't have started. It seems we've almost said that, if you want to be used of God, you have to be like a man instead of being like the woman about whom the book of Proverbs speaks.

I am not speaking of being great, such as in the history books. We're not striving for that kind of notoriety; I am speaking of being great in the areas of how we serve the man of God, how we serve one another, and how we serve the Lord Jesus Christ.

The person who will practice Philippians 4:6, which says, *"Be careful for nothing; but in every thing by prayer and supplication with thanksgiving let your requests be made known unto God,"* will then have the promise of verse 7, *"And the peace of God, which passeth all understanding, shall keep your hearts and minds through Christ Jesus."*

Back to my operation! I wore a neck collar for quite a while. Soon after I had the first operation, I leaned over, and a disc in my back went out. The doctors again decided I should wait on having surgery. I went through all kinds of treatment, and of course, the operation was the last resort, but finally, it had to be that. By that time, God had blessed and had been with me in such a way that there seemed to be no problem.

What are you going to have to face? There were about five years involved in this particular health dilemma, and I was very limited. I had to think about, "When do I take my medicine? When do I have my operation? How much can I do after my operation? How many hours will I be in bed? For how many weeks?" All the emphasis was placed on sickness.

Get ready! I don't know what you will have to face. I don't wish any of this for you, but some of you will face so much more than God has allowed me to face so far; to you I can say that God blesses through sickness.

I can say that what He has allowed me to have has been a blessing to me, and it has helped me. Whatever He wants in your life, then you want it, too! We don't seek suffering, but neither should we shun it. We might have to have it to work in us the work that He wants us to perform, or that He wants to perform through us. Be ready for whatever He allows to come into your life.

People will be astounded and question, "What is the matter with you? What is the matter with that girl? What is the matter with that woman? She doesn't understand what the problem is; she acts like nothing is happening."

Then you could say, "No, it is not like that at all! I do understand, but for me, God is opening a 'Red Sea.' " Just like God parted the Red Sea for the children of Israel fleeing a wrathful Pharaoh, God will part the Red Sea for us! There are many reasons for troubles, and He might allow them in your life. Just remember, you are going toward God's will in your life. Keep your eyes on the goal instead of the troubles. He will part the Red Sea for you so that you can walk straight toward

His goal for you!

Really, we have no problems! We, as Christians, do not have problems! Don't even say, "I'm nervous! I'm just the nervous type." No! Just say, "I don't get upset." If you do or don't, say, "I don't get upset! Christians don't get upset."

How God could use some Christian women who do not get upset! Some women are needed who do not fling themselves around saying, "I've got this problem. You just don't understand about my problems." No lady is going to come to that kind of woman to share her problems and seek help.

There Is Nothing that Can Touch You Except It Be Allowed by the Will of God for Your Good and His Glory!

It is as if you are in a great big balloon. I don't know what the fad is called, but I read about people riding in these giant balloons. In my mind, I feel that each person has his own balloon and floats around through the air. To me, it feels like we are in a big, protected covering. Nothing can penetrate to us except it be for our good and His glory. Nothing can penetrate through that balloon except it be allowed by the will of God.

When we realize this wonderful truth, then we have no problems because anything that comes to us is not a problem; it is a blessing from God. As we receive it that way, God will work through it. We will not be able to believe what He can do through us if we believe this.

People will say, "How did she do that? Her husband has just died and look! She is smiling." It is the funeral, and she is sitting there smiling through tears. She can say, "It's Jesus!"

The world says, "I can tell you what is happening and what is going to happen. She's under some kind of drugs; and in three or four days, she will go to pieces." I know so many ladies about which this is not true. They never did go to pieces. Of course, they missed their husbands, and as they honored God, they honored their husbands. It is natural for a widow to miss her husband. It would be terrible if she didn't miss him. "...*Ye sorrow not, even as others which have no hope.*" (I Thessalonians 4:13b) Christians sorrow in a different way. We sorrow with tears and smiles at the same time. The world is not able to understand because it is Jesus living through us. *"And the peace of God, which passeth all understanding, shall keep your hearts and minds through Christ Jesus."* (Philippians 4:7)

You say, "How? How can I do this? I don't know how to start practicing. I don't live this way."

All right, let me share the "how." Make Philippians 4:8 your verse: *"Finally, brethren, whatsoever things are true, whatsoever things are honest, whatsoever things are just, whatsoever things are pure, whatsoever things are lovely, whatsoever things are of good report; if there be any virtue, and if there be any praise, think on these things."* You live it by letting your mind start thinking these good thoughts!! When a negative thought comes into your mind, you can't help that; negative thoughts are going to come into your mind. The world, the flesh, and the Devil are going to see to it that some negative thoughts hit your mind. However, as soon as those negative thoughts enter, grab one of those good thoughts..."*pure,*" "*good,*" "*lovely*"...and think on it. Only one thought at a time can occupy your mind. Grab a good thought...perhaps think about someone you have won to Christ or something you can do for someone. Put it in your mind, and it will drive away the negative thought. But you say, "I can do it for only a minute." Okay. Quickly get another thought and practice it day after day and finally those of you who know the Lord Jesus Christ will be able to *"Rejoice in the Lord alway: and again I say, Rejoice."*

God didn't say, "Rejoice in your troubles." I met a lady in a Baptist church in Chicago, Illinois, who had lost three children within three weeks. Her tragedy was a house fire in which she and her husband and two children escaped safely, but

The Prevention

three children died. I believe one of them died while coming through the flames to her; the other two died a week apart. A funeral was conducted in that church for three consecutive weeks for that family.

That dear lady said, "Mrs. Evans, seven years before that fire, I almost had a nervous breakdown. Since then I have accepted Christ. Now I've gone through all this...all praise to the Lord Jesus...in a way that people have said, 'How did you do it? What is it?' " Because of the way she handled her situation, she could point them to the Lord Jesus Christ.

Let me say again, **trouble comes to the saved and the unsaved, but the way in which we react to that trouble will determine if we gain the attention of the world.** If we don't react any differently than the world is reacting, then there is nothing for them to notice so that they come to us and ask, "Hey! How come? What?" There is no way we can point them to Jesus.

Things seem to be shaping up for troubles that will be worse and worse as far as economics are concerned. If we are ready and live through the problems we have in our own lives, people are going to say, "How?" and we can point to the Lord Jesus. Folks will be coming to us, knocking our doors down saying, "How? How do you live like this?" If we are not living through problems, rejoicing in the Lord always, and we are just like everyone else, we will be of no help.

Let me say, if you have had some kind of nerve problem or some organic problem, I know nothing about that. I know there are some people who have nerve problems and need to go to the doctor, and they need the help God can give them through technology, through the great treatments that God has helped doctors to learn and to know. But many doctors will say that most of us can have this thing controlled right in our own minds. I believe we can if we have the Lord Jesus in our lives. If you do not know Jesus, of course, you had better worry! You had better be depressed! You have every right and every reason in the world to be upset.

If you have the Lord Jesus as your Saviour, you have no problems; you should not get upset! My Sunday school teacher kept telling me, "Oh, no, Christians don't get upset!"

I said, "I do."

But she kept telling me this over and over again, giving me the verses, giving me Philippians 4:4-8 and also Romans 8:35-39. I memorized them. I've said them over and over again. *"Who shall separate us from the love of Christ? shall tribulation, or distress, or persecution, or famine, or nakedness, or peril, or sword? As it is written, For Thy sake we are killed all the day long; we are accounted as sheep for the slaughter. Nay, in all these things we are more than conquerors through him that loved us. For I am persuaded, that neither death, nor life, nor angels, nor principalities, nor powers, nor things present, nor things to come, Nor height, nor depth, nor any other creature, shall be able to separate us from the love of God, which is in Christ Jesus our Lord."* Then what can separate us or hurt us? Nothing! Nothing can hurt us! Nothing can touch us except it be allowed by the will of God for our good and for His glory.

You say, "I read the Bible, and it doesn't mean anything to me." If you read it as literature, it won't mean anything to you. However, stop and think about each word. For example, in Romans 8:35 stop on the word *"famine"* and think about it. Just talk back and forth to the Lord when you have your devotions. When you come to the part about famine, you can say, "Oh, Lord, be with those people in India and Africa who are just waiting for death, sitting patiently, stoically waiting for death. God, I don't know why. I don't understand why You've allowed me to be here in this country where I have all the food I want! I don't understand it!" You have just talked with God. He has talked to you about famine, and you've talked to Him about famine.

Then think of those who have to face being persecuted and people who have no clothes. Remember, there are people who have lost their jobs. Their names will be recalled to your mind, and it might be that, when you are through, you will look at your prayer list and say, "Lord, just a minute; let me see if there is anyone I've left out." Perhaps you've done that with a friend. Sometimes I write down what I want to talk to a person about, and when I talk to him, I'll say, "Let me look over the things I've been writing down to tell you so that I won't omit anything."

Let the Lord Talk to You Through His Word!

There is a special joy in letting the Lord talk to you and your talking to Him. He will remind you of your prayer list as you go through these verses of Scripture. Other verses I have memorized are John 14:1–6: *"Let not your heart be troubled: ye believe in God, believe also in me. In my Father's house are many mansions...."* Now stop with that word, *"mansion."*

Say, "Lord, I remember that time when I went to visit a mansion. I remember when my family took me to see the Stephen Foster mansion. In my mind, I can see that mansion. Lord, bless my brother who does not have a mansion in the sky." This kind of conversation is so natural. You are reminded from the Word of God to say something to Him about someone who is not saved. Maybe your trip to see a mansion was with school kids, and that reminds you that some of them aren't saved and that they don't have mansions. Maybe you will sit and recall the front porch pillars, the furniture, and the clothes, and then say, "But Lord, that is nothing compared to the mansion You have made for me in Heaven. Thank You, Lord! I love You, Lord, for that mansion."

This kind of talking back and forth is comfortable, and God will work through it. The more you get into the Word, the more the Word gets into you, and this kind of talking will become an important part of your life!

I believe nerves, worry, depression, a critical spirit, gossiping, and griping all go together! I don't know which of them is in your life, but nerves, worry, and depression bring on gossiping and griping! If you are depressed when you see others doing something, you want to criticize them. Criticizing then brings on nerves, worry, and depression. If you are nervous, you are going to become depressed.

Certainly, there are many reasons for Christian women to become depressed. All afternoon, we sit and watch programs such as, "As the World Whirls," or "As the Stomach Churns," or "John's Other Wife." Then we wonder why we are depressed! When the time comes to make supper that night, we say, "I'm so exhausted. I don't know what is the matter with me. I'm so tired!"

I can tell you what the matter is with you. You have lived through three abortions, two affairs, and six drug addiction cases, and you're worn out. You are literally worn out emotionally. We feed the wrong things into our minds and then expect not to be nervous, worried, or depressed. Of course, we are going to be nervous, worried, and depressed.

We have just briefly discussed two of what I believe are the five sins of Christian women: (1) Nerves, worry, and depression, and (2) Gossip and a critical spirit. The other three are: (1) Immodest dress, (2) Lack of loving your husband and children, and (3) Lack of soul winning, Bible, and prayer.

You retort, "There are plenty of other sins. What about the sin of not taking care of our children and home?"

All right, that is a good point. However, if you love your husband, you are trying to work out a way to take care of your children. At least, you are going to want to keep a path cleared through the house so your husband can walk through it when he comes home. I believe taking care of your children comes under the category of loving your husband.

The Prevention

You say, "What about reading your Bible! What about sins of omission—not attending church and not praying?"

I promise you, if you are having victory in the five areas I named, you will be reading your Bible, praying, and going to church.

All kinds of women will talk to you about having Bible study. We have a lot of Bible study, but we see women coming into Bible study who talk about giving their lives over to the Holy Spirit, and then they go right outside the door of that Bible study and begin gossiping, griping, and complaining. There are so few women who will say, "We have sins, women! We have sins in our lives, and I'm crying to you about it!"

I've asked God to help me to do that for women. Far too often the women speakers at most Mother-Daughter Banquets talk about how beautiful the rainbow is: "If we all work together, there will be red, yellow, blue, and purple. Let's be pretty like rainbows." And almost immediately after the audience gets through hearing about being pretty like the rainbow, they go out criticizing each other. What I am giving is completely different from most anything Christian women hear or read.

Let's Be Different from the Ordinary!

In order to be different from the ordinary, some of us need to talk about the sins of Christian women and ask God to help deliver us from them. "Let's be different women!" has been my plea. We must have some different women—some girls who are different from the ordinary! At Hyles-Anderson College where I work, I am praying that God will make me different from what I am now. God has helped me come a little way, but I know I need to come a lot further. I know what my goal is, and I won't turn to the right or to the left. I believe God will help me reach that goal.

I just wonder if it is possible to have a group of different women and girls. My dream is to have some girls who are not in college dormitories griping about one another and talking only about clothes and boys. At Hyles-Anderson College, we happen to have some classes on clothes. We think it is wonderful to be appropriate. A model learns to walk, sit, and stand just so she can sell clothes. On the other hand, our college young ladies are learning to walk, sit, and stand so they can be modest ladies. How important it is to place emphasis on being appropriate in dress and learning how to walk, sit, and stand.

It is also appropriate that we talk about boys. There is not a better place than a Christian college to find a Christian guy. That, in itself, is one of the most important reasons for a girl to attend a Christian college. (Certainly it is not the only reason, but it is an important one.) Christian guys attend Christian college, and she is going to marry **someone**. Please don't put that down as a reason by any means. Go where Christian boys are who love the Lord and who really want to serve Him. There are so many dormitories where all of the conversation centers on clothes and boys.

We would like to think that it is possible for some girls to be praying for America—the country in which their children will be reared. We feel it is possible for some girls to think of something besides clothes and boys once in a while. Is it possible to have a school where they will say, "If a girl is from that school, you can count on her not to be gossiping, griping, whiney, and complaining"?

I don't know if that is possible. I've never seen it yet. I've never heard anyone say, "Isn't it something the way the girls at that school don't gossip, gripe, or complain!" Is that possible? I wouldn't mind even having some carbon copies of such girls. There are always certain characteristics that identify graduates from a certain school. Oh, that we might have some carbon copies, where they could say, "They are all like this: you can't get them to criticize. They are not critical, they are not gossipy, they don't gripe, and they don't complain!"

Different Girls and Different Women Are My Dream!

Oh, that is my dream! Could it be possible? All things are possible with God. If girls decide, one by one, that this is the kind of girl they want to be, then they are going to be!

I have actually had people say to me in private, "I don't respect women!" They quickly add, "To do anything for God, I believe you have to be a man or act as a man acts." Those people make those statements because they haven't had any respect for women. Let's covenant to turn the tide! Be the kind of woman whom girls can respect! They need to see that you can be something for God as well as keep the role of a lady. You can be a Christian lady really being used of God.

Preachers' wives, would it be possible to have a group of girls in your church who are different from the ordinary? Or do the girls in your church gossip? Perhaps they have their own little clique. Oh, it is a Christian clique, where they gossip in a "Christian" way. I'm afraid too much of the time that is exactly what we have. We don't separate from the world; we just take the world into the church and act the same way as the world acts. Let's not look down our noses at women of the street. Let's not look down our noses at alcoholics and drug addicts. Let's think about what **our** faults are!

You say, "Lord, I don't want to be nervous, worried, and depressed. I want to be a victorious, happy Christian." I believe He has shown us in the Word of God how we can be delivered **if** we will practice it. We will have to pay the price of disciplining ourselves by practicing thinking on those things that are holy, true, just, lovely, and pure.

PART TWO

*The Diagnosis
of the Five Sins of Christian Women*

CHAPTER ONE

Nerves, Worry, and Depression

> "Don't tell me worry doesn't do any good. I know better. The things I worry about don't happen!"
> –Anonymous

Perhaps we don't really know how we are guilty of showing ourselves nervous, worried, or depressed. So often one of these three—nerves, worry, or depression—is the real culprit when people show their temper through:
1. **Short answers.** For example, when a question is asked, the person replies, "It doesn't matter to me. I could care less."
2. **No answer.** For example, when a question or a statement requiring a comment is asked, the person's response is stony silence as if the person is deaf.
3. **Withdrawal.** For example, the person turns on his heel and marches to his room to meditate in silence or stands among people just gazing into space.
4. **Curt commands.** For example, a worker asks a question about how to do a particular part of the project. The person in charge tersely answers, "Just get it done...I don't care how...just do it!"
5. **Angry body English.** For example, the person tears through a screen door without opening it.
6. **Angry or cool facial expressions.** For example, the person angrily curls his lip, rolls his eyes, wrinkles his nose, or furrows his brow.
7. **Angry movements toward machines.** For example, the person kicks the washing machine, bangs on a computer, or jerks the car from lane to lane while driving.
8. **Verbal tirades.** For example, the person uses "Christian" cursing and makes statements such as "That fathead, dumb driver! What in the world does he think he's doing?"

Nervousness causes us to do stupid things which get us into a heap of trouble and sometimes tragedy. Richard Speck, the notorious killer of Chicago nurses, said that every one of the nurses would be alive if one of the girls hadn't spit in his face when he and his drugged cohorts tried to rob them. We'll probably never know whether or not that was true.

"He that keepeth his mouth keepeth his life: but he that openeth wide his lips shall have destruction." Proverbs 13:3 certainly has been true over and over again and is a wise saying from the Word of God. In this day of rejected people, who feel they are born losers, a slurred remark is enough to touch off a murderous spark in their oftentimes drunken or doped minds.

People Under Pressure

In today's society, we seem to talk as if we are under more pressure than women of other times. We talk about juggling two careers, living in a pressure cooker, and burnout as very real possibilities waiting just around the corner to pounce on every woman.

Sometimes people look at the farmer's wife of the past, thinking her life was easy without today's pressure. I lived in farming country, and I never did see one of those ladies living without pressure. They searched the skies and studied the calendars and almanacs trying to figure out whether or not they were going to get the right crops in and out of the ground at the right time in order to make a living. They snatched their livelihood from the land under terrific pressure. The ones who thought about it all of the time were nervous, worried, negative, cynical, and depressed just like the woman under pressure today. They had no more peace than we sometimes do, even though we should know the promise of John 14:27, *"Peace I leave with you, my peace I give unto you: not as the world giveth, give I unto you. Let not your heart be troubled, neither let it be afraid."*

When I have been traveling with other people, I have often seen someone sitting on a porch of a poor, little, rundown shack. I have heard others comment, "That must be the life—no worries, no pressure." The people I know who have

Nerves, Worry, and Depression

little to do, little for which to hope, and little of real value about which to think feel very pressured and have the high blood pressure and early strokes and heart attacks to prove it. If you are not in a pressure cooker, you will make one some way or another. These ladies, who seemingly are not achieving anything, spend their time trying to juggle gossip and soap operas, and they are sitting on the porch singing a "Somebody-Done-Somebody-Wrong" song. That kind of life causes boredom, and boredom causes fatigue, and fatigue causes depression. That's a woman under pressure.

The achiever drives past the shack and gives her "must-be-nice" commentaries, and the woman on the porch in the rocker watches the one driving by appearing to be going places and says, "Now, that's the life—air-conditioned car, music, and fancy clothes. It must be nice."

The homemaker working outside the home knows she's under pressure. The homemaker at home sometimes says "Yes!" to so many outside-the-home projects and expects perfection of herself to the point that she feels guilty if she ever sits down to relax. If she isn't a woman under pressure, she feels she isn't living right.

Single women sometimes feel that they'd better be achievers as they have nothing to use as an excuse for not being superhuman.

Whether or not we are alone, widowed, separated, divorced, or married; whether or not we are married and without children or with one, two, three, or six babies, small children, or grown children; we can find ways to put ourselves into the pressure cooker.

Now, if you are interested in staying out of the "pressure-cooker syndrome" that brings on depression, I have some ideas.

1. Learn to say "No" in an acceptable way. We say "Yes" to things we don't want to do, should not do, and to things our family, pastor, boss, nor anyone else cares whether or not we do. There are things we do not want to do that we should make ourselves do for our own good or for the good of our jobs, churches, or people close to us. I am not talking about that. I am talking about the number of times we say "Yes" simply because we do not know how to say "No."

One thing is, don't just say "No." In fact, you might not have to use the word. When someone asks you to do something, you can say how you wish it were possible; then give him ideas or help him think of someone who never gets asked to do anything. Then wind up by saying, "Maybe I can help you next time." There's not a "NO" in all of that conversation. You might have helped the asker get someone who really wanted to do the job, gotten a job for someone who truly needs more to do, and left the door open for you to help at a later time. Do not say "Yes" simply because you do not know how to say "No."

Pressure can be good, and we sometimes work at our best under some pressure and still have peace. But we do not have to live in a pressure cooker and be the woman under pressure.

2. Learn that it might be best for everyone if you do not always do your best. Sometimes we do our very best on a meal only to be so aggravated at everyone that nobody enjoys the meal. Serving a meal with fewer items or of less flavor would have been your best in that case. *"Better is a dry morsel, and quietness therewith, than an house full of sacrifices with strife."* (Proverbs 17:1)

3. Rejoice over your sister's achievements and do your best—not your sister's best. If your sister or sister-in-Christ is good at handcrafts and you are not, rejoice for her and do not put yourself under pressure to do what she does. Relax and do better at being what God wants you to be. *"Rejoice in the Lord alway: and again, I say, Rejoice."* (Philippians 4:4)

Nerves, Worry, and Depression

Ladies, Worry and Fear Can Paralyze!

When I was in my early 30's, a Tennessee Temple College student who was a photographer for *The Chattanooga News Free Press* took a picture of my children and me for the cover of the weekend magazine at Halloween time. David, Joy, nor I were scared of Halloween at all—puzzled, interested, nervous, or excited, but we were not afraid. We knew there weren't any "goblins" that would get us if we didn't watch out when we looked at the jack-o-lanterns.

You are probably not scared of goblins either, but what are your worries and fears? I have known ladies who were terrified of crossing bridges or railroad tracks, flying in airplanes, going to sleep, death, sickness, mice, strange or even familiar noises, thunderstorms, lightning, wind, certain people, crowds, doctors, walking alone into a room, water, elevators, rejection, guns, heights, closed-in places, loneliness, snakes, spiders, animals, dark mountain curves—you name it.

When my husband and I were in our early married years, we rented a room in an old house in the woods for $2.00 per week. It had no basement or foundation, and the whole place was full of mice! We had kitchen privileges, so I would sweep once in a while. When I picked up the broom one time, three mice scurried away in all directions. I got to be quite nervous with "mouse mania."

We were both cozily asleep in our big feather bed one night when I heard a "scratch, scratch, scratching" which seemed to be coming from one window protected only by screens. In the pitch dark, I could imagine a man climbing in over the window sill ready to club us to death for our millions. I sat up and screamed bloody murder.

My husband doesn't waken too quickly, so he just lay and groaned. When I heard his groan, I knew someone had gotten him, and I screamed again. We must have spent ten minutes screaming and groaning at each other before we were awake enough to discover a mouse playing around with papers in the dresser drawer!

It helps to identify your worries and fears. Many people—even Christians on their way to Heaven—think they are afraid of death. Now, really, who could be afraid of golden streets, no tears, and meeting Jesus face to face? We might want to stay on earth a while yet and still have Heaven to look forward to, but afraid or worried? Not really! I think we are afraid of how we might die more than the actual death. I am afraid I might lose my mind and my Christian testimony through intense pain on the way to death. Death for a Christian is nothing to fear: *"O death, where is thy sting? O grave, where is thy victory?"* (I Corinthians 15:55)

When you stop to think about it, doing things to lose your testimony because of pain loses its fear, too, when you think of I Corinthians 10:13, which says, *"There hath no temptation taken you but such as is common to man: but God is faithful, who will not suffer you to be tempted above that ye are able; but will with the temptation also make a way to escape, that ye may be able to bear it."*

It's wonderful to know the peace of God that comes from His Word. *"When thou liest down, thou shalt not be afraid: yea, thou shalt lie down, and thy sleep shall be sweet."* (Proverbs 3:24) It really is impossible to lie in bed afraid when you are quietly going over verses like: *"For God hath not given us the spirit of fear; but of power, and of love, and of a sound mind."* (II Timothy 1:7)

"Let not your heart be troubled…" (John 14:1)

"Peace I leave with you, my peace I give unto you: not as the world giveth, give I unto you. Let not your heart be troubled, neither let it be afraid." (John 14:27)

"The LORD is my shepherd; I shall not want. He maketh me to lie down in green pastures: he leadeth me beside the still waters. He restoreth my soul: he leadeth me in the paths of righteousness for his

Nerves, Worry, and Depression

name's sake. Yea, though I walk through the valley of the shadow of death, I will fear no evil: for thou art with me; thy rod and thy staff they comfort me. Thou preparest a table before me in the presence of mine enemies: thou anointest my head with oil; my cup runneth over. Surely goodness and mercy shall follow me all the days of my life: and I will dwell in the house of the LORD for ever." (Psalm 23)

Sometimes I have to make up things that might happen in the future in order to have something about which to worry. Phrases and short sentences from Psalm 37 can help us get control over these fears we women have. *"Fret not," "Trust in the LORD," "Commit thy way unto the LORD," "Rest in the LORD," "Wait patiently for him," "Cease from anger," "Forsake wrath,"* and *"Fret not thyself."*

Come to think of it, perhaps the goblins of fear and worry will get us if we don't watch out! We can watch out by making a study of the fear nots, fret nots, and be not afraid verses in the Bible. Look them up in your concordance, write them out, and put them all around you, memorize them, and let the Lord love you through them. He will chase away those goblins!

Right Responses
to Nerves, Worry, and Depression

People, let's learn to have right responses during times of nerves, worry, and depression. We don't need to react and cause further hurts.

1. **Show nothing and say nothing.** Tell yourself, "I will not help anything the way I feel right now."

2. **Write down the offense without anyone seeing, and hopefully, in a way no one understands but you.** Deal with it when going through paperwork.

3. **Be philosophical about the offense.** Make statements to yourself like, "It will all come out in the wash." "We haven't seen the last chapter." "I was upset about something similar last year, and it all worked out fine." "I need to find another

way to teach that." "How did I give instructions on that matter?"

4. **Immediately start complimenting a positive.** For example, say, "You are such a beautiful person. Your eyes are so sparkly." "I love that color on you." Suppose a weight watcher gains weight instead of losing weight. That would certainly be depressing. Making a statement like, "Your eyes are so beautiful," will take off the pressure and perhaps help that person to be able to formulate a new plan.

5. **Start asking questions galore which will point to a solution when faced with a problem.** Do not allow anyone to take much time assigning the blame to herself or anyone else on the spot. Quickly relieve any guilty persons so they can be free to find a quick solution. Nothing can bring on worry and depression like being blamed for a situation that is out of our control.

6. **Register the problem only if it seems to be a pattern.** Even then, reject the problem if you have already found you do not have enough control to reach a solution. Spinning wheels on a problem that will have to work itself out is putting unnecessary wear and tear on the body and mind.

7. **Get alone as soon as possible in order to complain to God.** However, turn slowly from people involved in the situation to avoid their being hurt.

8. **Read Psalms until your soul and spirit are quieted.** Read until your mind is on the possible.

9. **Go alone and cry rather than nagging and harping.** Tears cried in private for relief are a wonderful gift of God. Take advantage of that outlet.

Usually, we are most demonstrative about the negative and most philosophical about the positive. Instead, let's be philosophical about the negative and demonstrative about the positive. Many families who make statements like, "We're just

Nerves, Worry, and Depression

not the demonstrative kind," are surely demonstrative when it comes to something bad happening.

Nothing takes a toll on the human body, soul, and spirit quite like nerves, worry, and depression. For that reason, we must depend on our faith in God to help us overcome nerves, worry, and depression about any matter in life.

CHAPTER TWO

Gossip, and Critical Thinking

> *"Criticism
> can only destroy us if
> we respond incorrectly."*
> –Dr. Jack Hyles

I HAVE HAD PEOPLE actually ask, "What is gossip?" And I honestly think some people do not know. Let me share some of my definitions.

• **Gossip is the giving of bad reports that are true or untrue.** *"A talebearer revealeth secrets: but he that is of a faithful spirit concealeth the matter."* (Proverbs 11:13)

• **Gossip is idly chattering about the problems of our own family members.** The chatter may be true, but we would be surprised how few would know it if we did not tell it, and if "everyone" should know it, they don't have to know it from our mouths.

Sometimes we even spread the word on ourselves and then bring great harm to our own name. For example, I once counseled with a girl about a suspicion of stealing in connection with her name. She promptly went to friends to tell them of the incident. The friends, in turn, told other friends. Later, when something was taken, people decided it was the girl who had been called into my office. As far as I know, the girl has never stolen, but I wonder if there won't be an incident ten years from now when some 30-year-old lady says, "You know, I cannot remember all of the details, but I think something happened about her and stealing back in college." It is very possible this young girl's idle chatter could lose her a job someday.

Often, we are the ones who keep the fire burning, and then we wonder how the further word got out. We ourselves told it! *"My heart was hot within me, while I was musing the fire burned: then spake I with my tongue."* (Psalms 39:3)

• **Gossip is telling our feelings about things we do not like or about which we do not agree.** Why bother giving our little, puny opinions? Within a few months or years, we no longer hold to that opinion anyway. Of course, we are not referring to Bible doctrines in this point.

- **Gossip is sharing those "stupid" things husbands do.** Be sure not to tell the girlfriends anything about your husband that you would not want him to tell the boys about you. By the way, those girlfriends think you are pretty stupid for choosing a husband who does such "stupid" things.

After we are over our little miff, a girlfriend refers to our husband in a displeasing way, and we are ready to fight her—forgetting we are the one who weakened him in front of her!

- **Gossip is telling your financial status to anyone but God or one godly counselor.**

I have just been wondering if we, who think we know what gossip is and think we do not gossip, really know what it is. It is giving forth bad reports—true or untrue.

Who Is a Gossip?

A gossip is merely one who is a bearer of bad reports. The reports she speeds along may not be true, but they are bad opinions and complaints. The opinions she glibly throws out do not characterize the one who has the law of kindness in her tongue. They are bad reports. The words the gossip spits at you may be about herself or her own, but they are still bad reports!

Beware! Stay away! She will kill your spirit, numb your heart, and paralyze your brain.

Watch for cute little remarks with double meanings, syrupy prayer requests with lifts of the eyebrow, or shrugs of the shoulders. Some gossips give their best performances in a way which would keep you from knowing who hit you where and when. You just know you heard something, but you cannot quite place the occasion of the unloading of the "garbage truck."

I repeat, a gossip is merely a purveyor of bad reports. They are her speciality.

To Gossip or Not to Gossip!

Have you ever found yourself in a situation where you are just about to join in the gossip? Someone has started to gossip, and you feel yourself about to ask a choice question which will lead to more conversation.

What are you to do? Perhaps you say to yourself, "I should not say anything, but I've just got to ask this question."

You really think about it; you full well know what you are doing, but you still go ahead! Sometimes I have done exactly that! Sometimes afterward, it comes to me that I was a gossip. We are so used to gossip and a critical spirit that we don't even see it! It is just so much a part of us that it is something we do all the time. I know this fact is true, for sometimes I'll say to a student, "I heard you said this."

"Really?" she asks. "You mean that matters?"

We wrongly feel that this is the way women are or the way women are supposed to be!

It is shocking to me how, for some reason, the church house seems to have become a safe harbor for those who gossip. Many churches have socials where they plan for women to gossip. They might as well say, "Now the men will be doing such and such, and the women can come, bring their sewing, and do their gossiping over in the corner." Or, they should advertise, "The women can read dirty books." Doing so is laughable! Yet, that is how we treat gossip! It is not considered a sin, and it causes more trouble in churches and in Christian homes than all the liquor, all the dirty books, and anything else of which you can think! Because gossiping is our personal pet sin, we overlook it. We understand what we mean by it!

Spreading Gossip Through Prayer Requests?

Often, we even try to dignify gossip by saying, "It's because we want you to pray more intelligently for the person. I'm just giving a prayer request." While you are giving the prayer request, you state, "John and Mary are in trouble, and I think what has been happening is that John has been going out with someone's wife!" We sound like a television serial giving a prayer request! All we have to say is, "Please pray for John and Mary," and we really don't even have to give the names; God knows to whom we are referring. Just say, "There is a marital problem for which I want prayer." If you are not really spreading gossip, then be careful how you handle your prayer requests!

The reason I often ask for prayer through an "unspoken request" rather than in an open public announcement is because I do not trust human nature. Galatians 6:8 says, *"For he that soweth to his flesh shall of the flesh reap corruption; but he that soweth to the Spirit shall of the Spirit reap life everlasting."* Romans 8:5 adds, *"For they that are after the flesh do mind the things of the flesh; but they that are after the Spirit the things of the Spirit."* Even saved people, including **myself**, are sometimes more led by the world, the flesh, and the Devil than we are by the Holy Spirit. *"For all that is in the world, the lust of the flesh, and the lust of the eyes, and the pride of life, is not of the Father, but is of the world."* (I John 2:16)

These are my fears about giving some types of prayer requests to more than one person. Sometimes you can find one person who has a reputation for going only to God with requests and even then that person can slip into talking.

1. I fear reaping everyone's opinion about what I should do regarding a prayer request given.

2. I fear being judged for going against the opinion given me by an individual. *"But with me it is a very small thing that I should be judged of you, or of man's judgment: yea, I judge not mine own self. For I know nothing by myself; yet am I not hereby justified: but he that judgeth me is the Lord."* (I Corinthians 4:3–5)

3. I fear that I might be overly influenced by people who

have a more powerful way than most in expressing their opinion. I remember this fact being especially true when I was physically weak and deciding on the proper course of treatment for cancer.

4. I fear gossip about why a certain thing is happening to me.

5. I fear others' wanting to discuss my problem with me every time they see me, which keeps my mind focused on a problem and keeps me from functioning well.

6. I fear people discussing my problems with each other more than with God, which keeps them and me from Philippians 4:8 kind of thinking. *"Finally, brethren, whatsoever things are true, whatsoever things are honest, whatsoever things are just, whatsoever things are pure, whatsoever things are lovely, whatso-ever things are of good report; if there be any virtue, and if there be any praise, think on these things."*

7. I fear people's inability to divorce my problem from me (once my problem is solved), which will keep me from getting back on my feet, as I'm paralyzed when around people whom I know are still thinking of me in terms of my problem.

People, let's give more unspoken prayer requests. I believe more gossip is spread in churches in the name of the Lord than we are aware of! Believe me, God can bless prayer that is prayed by people who do not know the circumstances and therefore cannot pray "more intelligently" as well as He can answer our prayers when we don't know what to pray. *"Likewise the Spirit also helpeth our infirmities: for we know not what we should pray for as we ought: but the Spirit itself maketh intercession for us with groanings which cannot be uttered."* (Romans 8:26) Now, on the other hand, if we have been entrusted with the details of a prayer request, let's guard those details with our very lives and give the request to God only, guarding our own selves from pronouncing judgment even in

The Five Sins of Christian Women

our own minds and hearts. "*Casting down imaginations, and every high thing that exalteth itself against the knowledge of God, and bringing into captivity every thought to the obedience of Christ.*" (II Corinthians 10:5)

Spreading Gossip in Sunday School?

Sometimes gossip occurs right outside the Sunday school department door! Some of us constantly bemoan the fact that we don't have enough time to give individual attention to our Sunday school class members. Yet, we continue to use part of the precious minutes we do have reporting and sharing the latest news with another Sunday school teacher. We do this right outside the department or classroom, or would you believe, right in the Sunday school classroom!

Those few minutes could be used to talk to our Sunday school students as they come into the room. In fact, we might have as much as 20 to 30 minutes to visit with the very early arrivals. We might be used to win one person to Christ as we have time to find out that one is unsaved. We could be used to give some statements in a way which would begin to change a life. We could listen—really listen—and be the reason for someone having a better week. We could also conduct some pre-session activity which would keep the interest of someone who would then return the next Sunday. We could and should do anything but gossip!

Spreading Gossip in Circles?

Gossip in circles? I'm speaking of the Women's Missionary Society circles. The first time I visited a general Women's Missionary Society meeting in First Baptist Church, Hammond, Indiana, I heard the leader saying words my ears could not believe. First, I stared; and then, I embarrassed myself laughing, no, cackling out loud!

Gossip and a Critical Spirit

She was telling the ladies that they were to leave the homes in which the circle meetings were being held during the new year at a specific time of the evening. She said something like this, "Your business will be over by then, you will have had time for real fellowship, and your husbands and children will want you home soon after that time. Anything done after that time will probably deteriorate into a gossip session anyway."

I could almost trace the pattern that she was talking about, for I know too well. I had attended 100 such meetings, and I had taken part in the gossip-session time. Of course, the gossip had been "blessed" because we had opened our meeting with prayer. I guess that made it "sanctified" gossip.

The leader even had instructions for one whose circle met in her own sister-in-law's house: "If you want to stay with your sister-in-law a while after the meeting, you leave when the other ladies leave; drive around the block and then return. Then your husband can't blame the Women's Missionary Society for your not getting out on time."

You would have to know the leader, which I feel I do, and then you still would not understand what part was serious and what part was tongue in cheek on all these instructions. One thing for sure: she had our number! We women are gossips! And we really don't mind at all doing our gossiping in the name of church work! In fact, I am not even sure we know what gossip is.

I finally looked it up in the dictionary, and such words as, "idle tattler; a news monger," are not the ones I want associated with me—at least not at a Women's Missionary Society meeting, do you?

Spreading Gossip in the Church Nursery?

Once during my husband's years in graduate school, I helped out by taking a paid job in a church nursery. The $5.00

per Sunday I received paid for half of our weekly groceries. I thought I was rich in more ways than one. I loved caring for the babies, and I looked forward to having good fellowship with the nursery volunteers from among the church ladies.

I was in for a big surprise! Each lady seemed to reason: "Have opinion—will give." I had never heard the like in my life. When they got through filling me in, I realized that most of the babies had terrible mothers who didn't feed them well, didn't send enough diapers, weren't giving the right vitamins, and didn't spend enough time with them.

They talked about the baby who came to the nursery dirty. I don't think the baby's being dirty was as bad as our mouths spewing dirty words about the parents of the dirty baby. "*A naughty person, a wicked man, walketh with a froward mouth. He winketh with his eyes, he speaketh with his feet, he teacheth with his fingers; Forwardness is in his heart, he deviseth mischief continually; he soweth discord.*" (Proverbs 6:12–14)

I was very young and did not have children of my own yet. I really took in all these comments as the Gospel truth. In later years, I found out that this self-appointed position of pediatrician, social worker, pastor, judge, and jury is nothing more than holding the title, "bearer of bad reports." The attitude is one of a critical spirit.

There are few real exceptions. If there appears to be a case of child abuse, report it of course to the one in authority only. Let them take care of it.

One of the babies who was "not fed well enough" was just a dainty little girl. Later the pediatrician said she was in perfect health. The child who "did not have enough diapers," had a young mother who wasn't careful in her planning. She surely did show love for her young one.

On and on I could go, but enough said. I found that nursery workers are to take care of babies while their parents attend church. Period! That's all! It will relieve you who are nursery workers to know that you are not a teacher who has to give a grade on a report card for every parent of every child in your nursery. *"Walk in wisdom toward them that are without, redeeming the time. Let your speech be alway with grace, seasoned with salt, that ye may know how ye ought to answer every man."* (Colossians 4:5, 6) If you are truly burdened for some of the parents, open your mouth to God and shut your mouth to people. *"He that is void of wisdom despiseth his neighbour: but a man of understanding holdeth his peace. A talebearer revealeth secrets: but he that is of a faithful spirit concealeth the matter."* (Proverbs 11:12, 13)

Spreading Gossip in the Faculty Lounge?

I can remember being in the second grade in Mrs. Woods' class. She had sent all of us in her class out to the playground. I came back into the school to get the jump rope. Four teachers were standing outside the door of my room. They were talking about one of my friends and her family. I was crushed! I had gotten through kindergarten, first grade, and part of the second grade before I was disillusioned in this area.

Prior to this day, I am sure, I assumed that teachers were planning good things for us kids as they stood talking in the hallway together. Years later, I became a teacher. At times I happened to be one of four teachers talking together. We had nice rooms called "faculty lounges" in which to do our fellowshipping, relaxing, and planning together.

Once in a while, a student by mistake came in on us. Some kid once returned from the playground to get a jump rope. We wondered if she had overheard us. We were gossiping in the name of being interested in the kids.

Is your Christian school faculty lounge a room of sharing blessings, or is it a den of gossip? Would you want members of your family discussed in the same manner in which you and your colleagues freely discuss students and their families? Ask God to guard your mouth and ears in the faculty lounge.

Spreading Gossip at Christian Camps?

For some reason, the church house and church-related functions seem to become a safe harbor for those who gossip. Many, many young people tell me their life direction was changed toward the Lord's will at a camp or conference. Who can estimate the good that has been done in these wonderful environments of spirituality, fun, relaxation, fellowship, and retreat from the world! Let's be sure we women keep these camps and conference grounds free from the world. Oh, I know, we don't wear indecent or unladylike dress; we don't take beer or cigarettes on the Christian camp or conference grounds; but do we take a mind loaded with news and a mouth ready to tell it? What causes us to think that it is any better to take a foul mouth to camp than a cigarette?

Sometimes workers on conference or campgrounds come home from their summer of Christian work soured on all Christians. They have spent all of their free time and some of their work time exchanging tales from every group of campers and leaders who attended each week. By the time the camp workers get home, "fill in" all their friends, and recuperate from experiencing the truckload of garbage received during the summer, they have wasted half their school year. The real tragedy is that some never recuperate!

Girls and women, let's be ladies in the way we use our mouths! "*My lips shall not speak wickedness, nor my tongue utter deceit.*" (Job 27:4)

"*The heart of the righteous studieth to answer: but the mouth of the wicked poureth out evil things.*" (Proverbs 15:28)

"*Set a watch, O LORD, before my mouth; keep the door of my lips.*" (Psalms 141:3)

Stop the Loose Talk!

Several older ladies of my generation have told me that they were taught to say "limb" instead of "leg" and were admonished not to mention publicly the word "hose" referring to stockings.

When I, a middle-aged woman, was growing up, I shamed my mother by talking about her pretty, new, navy-blue satin maternity slip before my uncle. (I was so excited about our new baby coming to our house.) At that time, pregnant women went into public for funerals and weddings of very special people in their lives; otherwise, they stayed at home, especially during the last couple of months of their "confinement."

As a little girl, I was completely flabbergasted when my great-grandmother told my mother in my hearing that a certain relative was going to be sick in September. It was news to me that one could schedule one's illnesses!

All of these examples might seem ridiculous to me until I keep my mouth quiet and just listen to the conversations of young adults and teenagers from fundamental Christian homes and churches. Can there not be a balance? Are there not those things which are beautiful and right, but sacred and private? Before we start laughing too hard at the "older ways," let's take a good, hard look at the new ways. Most Christian men and women who are not married to each other do not discuss anatomy when they are working together. Why is it all right for the same two people to begin to discuss anatomy and all the ramifications of pregnancy after the woman is going to have a baby? If a dating couple believes in keeping certain intimacies special for marriage only, why is it all right to discuss certain days of the month so openly? Discussions of birth control methods seem to be commonplace with dating couples and mixed groups. I have even heard people refer to facts concerning their personal marriage relationship publicly. Many people think in pictures in this television age. Is this what we want? Do we want no private life at all? There is a lot to be said for such words as "discretion," "appropriateness," "diplomacy," and "tact." Why don't we think about these words before we laugh too hard?

Words Are Powerful!

If you must be around those who spout off their opinions as if their opinions were going out of style, you have to insulate yourself for survival. Try, with the help of God, to depersonalize every remark being tossed into the breeze. Usually, these gossips chatter idle words they can barely remember and for which they give no account. While you are home in bed "croaking," they are going on their merry way wondering, "What is the matter with poor, fragile Susie?" Often they actually have no idea Susie has been the victim of emotional abuse—by them!

Allow God to cleanse you through the washing of the Word of God. Keep a verse or verses handy in your pocket. Go over and over them in order to combat the feeling of hating everyone and everything as you live in the "fallout area." Refuse to feel guilty when you hear those with whom you live or work making statements such as "She just can't take it," or "I like someone around me I don't have to be careful about."

Everyone has to be careful with their words around everyone else. You are not the only one hurt by the words. You just happen to be the one who can be seen "burning out" on those words. Words are powerful. Words do influence—whether or not you want them to influence. Stay away from these words as much as possible. If you do have to live and work around them, refuse to dwell on them. *"Understanding is a wellspring of life unto him that hath it: but the instruction of fools is folly. The heart of the wise teacheth his mouth, and addeth learning to his lips. Pleasant words are as an honeycomb, sweet to the soul, and health to the bones. There is a way that seemeth right unto a man, but the end thereof are the ways of death. He that laboureth laboureth for himself; for his mouth craveth it of him. An ungodly man diggeth up evil: and in his lips there is as a burning fire. A froward man soweth strife: and a whisperer separateth chief friends. A violent man enticeth his neighbour, and leadeth him into the way that is not good. He shutteth his eyes to devise froward things: moving his lips he bringeth evil to pass. The hoary head is a crown of glory, if it be found in the way of righteousness. He that is slow to anger is better than the mighty; and he that ruleth his spirit than he that taketh a city."* (Proverbs 16:22–32)

Small Talk

Do you suppose we give out bad reports (true or false), tell things that are confidential, negative, or hurtful, or ask wrong questions because we do not know how to make small talk? We want to reach out to people and let them know we want to bridge the gap between them and us, but what are we to say? You don't just walk up to a casual acquaintance and ask, "Could we discuss the Ark of the Covenant in the Old Testament?" or "What do you think of our President's policy on foreign affairs?"

Our little depraved minds come out with something we think will make the other person feel good, such as, "Didn't Joe look stupid falling at the front of the church today?" That's it, we think. Say something to bring us together as we sit looking good while talking about a mutual acquaintance looking bad. *"Rejoice not when thine enemy falleth, and let not thine heart be glad when he stumbleth."* (Proverbs 24:17)

Or, we say something like, "It surely seems as if Martha is 'taking on' a long time over that miscarriage (or death of a loved one or divorce), doesn't it?" Really, we are just looking for something to say to reach out to one another.

In so doing though, we hurt the one whom we are discussing as well as the one to whom we are reaching. We are trying to take away a coat in the winter or cause an explosion. *"As he that taketh away a garment in cold weather, and as vinegar upon nitre, so is he that singeth songs to an heavy heart."* (Proverbs 25:20) We want to take the healing process away from the lady too fast. We want to sing songs, give Romans 8:28, and philosophize that it will all come out in the wash, before the sad person has had time to mourn.

While we are telling this to our "talking partner," we are preparing her to have heaviness of heart later as she gets to thinking about the unkind remarks made. Let's determine that our chatting not be heavy. *"But I determined this with myself, that I would not come again to you in heaviness. For if I make you sorry, who is he then that maketh me glad, but the same which is made sorry by me?"* (II Corinthians 2:1, 2) Just selfishly, for our own sake, we need to learn light, small talk.

With what words then can we reach out to bridge gaps? Words of comfort and edification are in order. *"Wherefore comfort yourselves together, and edify one another."* (I Thessalonians 5:11)

- "Wasn't that a good sermon?"
- "Have you ever heard that subject taught that way before?"
- "Mary sure sang that song well, didn't she?"
- "I believe spring is on the way, don't you?"
- "I hope you have a good weekend!" (Or vacation, day at work, Christmas, new year, Thanksgiving)
- "I've been praying for your mom. I heard she was sick."
- "Pretty day, isn't it?" (Or sunny, bright, clear, cool, warm, snowy, not-so-cold day even if overcast, less windy than yesterday, etc.)
- "That dress is pretty."

None of this small talk is earthshaking nor will it probably change lives, but the fact that you want to reach out to someone might be used of God to change a life. I know you might

Gossip and a Critical Spirit

get a negative response from some of your small talk, but you can learn to counteract that with further, positive small talk. Have a lot of interests and keep adding as some of them go by the wayside. Right now I'm interested in getting all my old pictures of my kids displayed all over my walls downstairs in my "Cracker Barrel" family room, as well as in my home study I call my "fruit cellar." I'm having a great time expanding my animal and bird watching into the hours after dark via my $12 spotlight. All of these give me things about which to talk that are not negative. I try not to end with talking about my interests either. Usually, the other person starts telling me about things that my interests have brought to their minds. *"Look not every man on his own things, but every man also on the things of others."* (Philippians 2:4) I'm glad for small talk, aren't you?

Are You Losing Control?

Can you feel when you are losing control through gossip or anger? Do you know when you are going to have a "hissy-fit"? (A "hissy-fit" is when someone decides she is going to have hysterics!) **You** personally decide to do it; there are very few who cannot stop it. You definitely decide whether or not you are going to let yourself go over the line. Here is an example of how a "hissy-fit" can happen: It is a very hot day; the kids are in the car. You have a flat tire and run out of gas on the freeway. Now what are you going to do? You let it build up and then you finally let go. You are in trouble, so you "RUN IN CIRCLES, SCREAM, AND SHOUT!" That is what you do!

Guess what? Your kids are watching you perform that way. They soon learn to say, "Momma is just that way!" Daughter thinks that is the way to be, and we just keep going generation after generation! I wonder, "Is it possible to have a different breed of women? A DIFFERENT breed of Christian women?" Do you know Christian husbands and wives have idle bickering and arguing as one of their sports, too? Oh, God, help us to be different from that!!

What do you do when you feel yourself losing control? Think of Proverbs 25:28, "*He that hath no rule over his own spirit is like a city that is broken down, and without walls.*" If a city doesn't have walls around it, it is vulnerable, it is weak, and anything can enter and take that city. Any enemy can take a person who has no walls around his spirit. Such people have no control over their own spirit. Remember Proverbs 16:32 says, "*He that is slow to anger is better than the mighty; and he that ruleth his spirit than he that taketh a city.*"

Perhaps you say, "I'm not going to let anyone tell me what to do! I'll stand up for my rights if anyone tries that on me!" The day comes when someone does ask you to do something, and then you look terrible in front of everyone who sees and hears you. They wonder how long it will be before you lose control of yourself and kill somebody.

I've been afraid that some little children that God has allowed me to teach would someday kill someone because they had no control over their own spirits. You wonder when they are grown up if someone will provoke them enough that they might attempt to kill someone. They show that the other person really has control over them. They are letting others dictate to them how they will act. What are you going to do if you cannot control your spirit?

You Can Control Your Spirit—Just Shut Up!

Shut up…
    about problems (whether or not they are widely known)
    about our family at home or our church family.
    about finances
    about things we do not like
    about stupid things our husbands do
    about stupid things our children (young or grown) do
    about stupid things our friends do

GOSSIP AND A CRITICAL SPIRIT

AND, MOST OF ALL,
about stupid things we do (unless it is a cute little joke on ourselves).
"But I determined this with myself, that I would not come again to you in heaviness." (II Corinthians 2:1) These are all bad reports and cause nothing but heaviness for us and for our listener. Shut up to people and talk to God! Let's quit our bad reporting! Let the media keep that as their business.

How to Escape the Trap of Gossip

I have had ladies come to me asking how to keep from gossiping when others around them seem to be declaring "open season" on people? I believe that God always provides an escape route. We just fail to look for it sometimes. *"Wherefore let him that thinketh he standeth take heed lest he fall. There hath no temptation taken you but such as is common to man: but God is faithful, who will not suffer you to be tempted above that ye are able; but will with the temptation also make a way to escape, that ye may be able to bear it."* (I Corinthians 10:12, 13)

Escape Routes

1. **As the conversation turns to criticism, say, "You know we should not be doing this. Let's see how many good things we can remember about this person."** Include yourself as if you were gossiping even if you have not entered into it yet. You don't want to hurt or squelch anyone as you want to help the gossiper just as much as you want to protect the one being attacked. After all, you just gossiped three days ago, remember?

2. **Change the subject completely, acting as if you haven't heard or had not been paying attention.** For example:
   • "Oh, look over there at Sue's dress. Isn't that a pretty color? Do you think she made it herself?" In this way you are programming the gossiper's next remarks

to be words of praise for someone.
- "Oh, I'm so sorry to hear that anyone thinks that about Mary. You don't believe it, do you?" You are inferring that, of course, the gossiper wouldn't stoop so low as to believe it.
- "If someone even thinks that about her, it makes me hurt for her. Let's pray for her right now." It will take the most confirmed gossiper to raise her head and say, "You know what else?"

3. ***If you cannot seem to be used to turn the tide of the conversation, RUN!*** Flee the Devil! *"Let no corrupt communication proceed out of your mouth, but that which is good to the use of edifying, that it may minister grace unto the hearers."* (Ephesians 4:29)

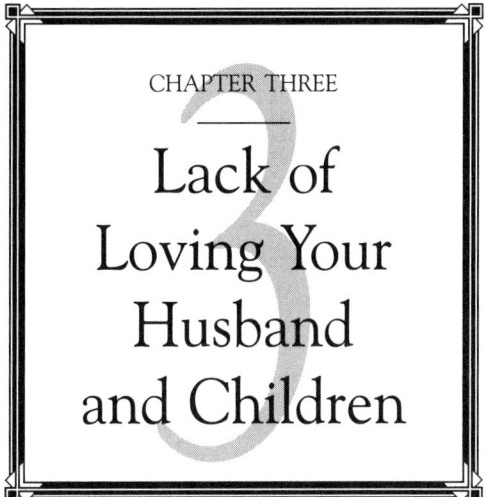

CHAPTER THREE

Lack of Loving Your Husband and Children

> "Just to love,
> that's enough;
> being loved,
> that's a bonus."
> –Dr. Jack Hyles

MOST OF US feel we are exempt from this one unless we run away from home, but that is just not so.

Let me precede my brilliant deductions on this subject by sharing what I hope is a parallel story. During the 1978 Pastors' School, our son David, who was in Hammond Baptist Junior High School, came home telling us, "We got flowers from Brother Hyles today, and they were beautiful! That shows where his heart is."

Yes, Preacher had sent a gorgeous basket of flowers to the school chapel to tell the kids he was still thinking of them even if thousands of people were visiting our church from across the nation.

I'm afraid we are not always that wise. We'll plan a big shower or special event for a Sunday school class or bus project but never think of doing anything different for our husband and children. I wonder how the kids feel when they see us going to all lengths for everyone but them!

We spend our lives keeping our children out of the goodies box prepared for someone else's children. That probably says a lot about where our hearts are. Those children we're chasing away from the beautiful handwork prepared for daily Vacation Bible School are the ones who will be planning or not planning for us when we are old.

Now, you know I think your projects of Christian service are wonderful and that your own children need to help you prepare and save for them, but must it be for others every time? Is it really right to save the good dishes for company—every time? Do you bake a special cake only for a funeral dinner? We must be emitting a message which really says where our heart is when we dress beautifully to go to a ladies' luncheon only to change to scroungy clothes for our husband and children.

When we're too busy to go to the basement to see about a junior-high science project, the message, "I really don't want to leave my thing to see yours," is transferred in red neon lights. Of course, you can't go THE minute every time, but maybe sometimes? When you can't go, does your child know you wish you could? We torture ourselves over planning that will not offend our friends. Do we plan how to avoid offending our own children? Where is the place where your heart is?

Remember when your husband used to ask you to go on business trips with him? How many times did you carelessly toss off, "Oh, no, I'm too busy," before he quit asking? You probably won't treat a friend that way.

Do you really love your husband and children so they know it? Be prepared! If you "go to the trouble" to be nice to your own, you'll be fought by a whole union. The members of that union won't want you to outshine them and thus put pressure on them. They will say, "I wouldn't go to all that trouble just for home folks." They will also die laughing when you plan happenings for your own family. They don't think it odd if it's for others, but just for you and your family?

Almost every married lady would declare, "I love my husband!" But do you really? Do you love him enough to obey him? Do any of the following statements fit you?

- "I love him, but I want him to be this way."
- "I'd like to see him change this and this."
- "I see some things where he doesn't exactly measure up. It is for his own good that I want him to change."

Wife, if you try to tell him what you want him to change in his life, he will decide that is exactly what he should keep! If he is a man, that is exactly what he is going to do! You don't want less than a man, do you? Or do you? Do you really want your husband to be like a little child whom you can boss?

You retort, "I don't boss my husband! I'm not the domineering type!" Okay, what did you do the last time he came in

Lack of Loving Your Husband and Children

and dropped his clothes on the floor? Let him decide whether or not he wants to drop his clothes on the floor. Did you ever stop to think that if you praised him for the things that you do like instead of spending all your time telling him what you don't like, God would bless you for it! Talk to a few widows and see what they say about just one more opportunity to pick up their husband's clothes.

Let's take what I call a "Bossy Woman Quotient Test." Check "yes" or "no" in the appropriate box.

❐ Yes ❐ No Do you find a way to see to it that you get what you want?

❐ Yes ❐ No Do you use the withholding of favors until you get what you think is coming to you?

❐ Yes ❐ No Do you use questions to attract attention to the mistakes of others?

❐ Yes ❐ No Do you suggest things until you get your way?

❐ Yes ❐ No Do you make light of another's work by criticizing anything that is not to your way of thinking?

❐ Yes ❐ No Do the children spontaneously say, "Dad is the boss"?

❐ Yes ❐ No Do you question decisions your husband makes without consulting you?

❐ Yes ❐ No Do you just sweetly chip away at a man's will until you get him to go your way without his ever knowing it?

❐ Yes ❐ No Do you ask questions of your parents, boss, or pastor until they just tell you to do it your way?

It's a dangerous thing to get your way all or most of the time. If you have the ability to get your way, it would be good to refrain from using it. You could win the battle and lose the war.

Are You Weakening Your Husband?

Have you decided you want a strong husband? As he tries to become stronger, do you weaken him? Do you realize what you are doing?

Far too many wives know how to make themselves pretty and coyly say to their husband, "You aren't going out soul winning again tonight, are you?" You know how to keep him home. Then you see that you keep him there, and he is weakened. After he is weakened, you have no respect for him, and then you don't want what you've helped to create. Ask God to keep you from making this kind of practice a part of your marriage.

Many a woman chips away at her boyfriend or husband, gets her way, and then ultimately loses the boyfriend or husband. Sometimes she does not lose her husband, but she wonders why she has such a weak husband. I know a teacher who in a cute way, changed her principal's mind several times each year and was surprised when she was fired.

There are times, when for the good of all concerned, you can talk over issues in a businesslike way. You know the difference between being a help and being bossy. So many times our main concern is just getting our own way—not helping anyone or anything. Who needs a bossy woman? Who wants to be a bossy woman? If the test caused you to think that you are a bossy woman, ask God for help from Him, His Word, and His people. *"Humble yourselves therefore under the mighty hand of God, that he may exalt you in due time."* (I Peter 5:6) *"Put them in mind to be subject to principalities and powers, to obey magistrates, to be ready to every good work."* (Titus 3:1)

"Gossipship" or Fellowship!

Yes, I am referring once again to that word "gossip." If we cared more about what our husbands and our preacher wanted us to do, we would be able to take better care of our chil-

Lack of Loving Your Husband and Children

dren. It all fits together. A preacher who really wants to serve the Lord is going to want to help you.

Are you ready to try to do whatever your preacher asks you to do? Some of you say, "But I don't want to hurt my home!" You are not worried about hurting your home! You are worried about hurting your telephone time. Some of you who are talking about all you are going to do all day long are not trying to learn how to do several things at a time and keep your sanity while you are doing it. You can learn to do several things at a time if you have a schedule and schedule your time! Check the time you spend on luncheons and committee meetings and out with the women of the church!

You say, "I've got to take care of my children." Are you really taking care of them or are you just *with* them? Do you take them with you everywhere you go and call that "spending time with them"? Do you ever leave your world and enter theirs and have fun just for them and with them? Or are you on the telephone, and the little kids are saying, "Hey, Mom! Hey, Mom!"

You shoo them away and say, "Just a minute! Just a minute!" That minute becomes 30 minutes! Are none of you guilty of that? Am I the only one who has done that?

Instead of making excuses, say to him, "Preacher, I don't know how I am going to do it. You are asking me to do something that I don't know how to do, but I want to find a way. Will you help me?"

Many times he can help you find a way to do the very thing that he has asked you to do! Maybe he has asked you to do some social project or help with a banquet. You say, "I just wouldn't have time for all my committee meetings." Give up the committee meetings! All you do is sit around and eat and talk and gossip. If you give up your meetings, then you might get the thing planned too!

You can have massive projects completed with a minimum

of planning just by letting one woman lead instead of a committee. This is her time to lead! Let her ask the ladies what they want to do. When a leader coordinates an event, it can be done with minimum of planning. Stop and think about the last time you planned something like a baby or bridal shower at the church. How many hours were spent planning? Was all that time actually needed? Was there a lot of "gossipship" along with fellowship in the planning of that shower?

By the way, when you plan a church shower, is it any different from a shower at a civic club or one planned by a public school faculty? Or is it a shower where the relatives of those people being honored come in, and they are completely left alone while church members talk about what happened in church last Sunday? Do we have our little cliques because we want to be with our own friends? Of course, we do. If you want to be a woman used of God, you'll have to give up that which you want! So you want to sit by Susie—don't! Whatever you want to do, there's a good chance you shouldn't do it! If what you want to do will not honor and bless others as they come to a church shower, don't do it!

What kind of a church shower do you have? Do you have a little devotional and a prayer so that you can say it was all right to be in a church? Do you know that I have been in public school facilities where they also had a prayer at a shower?

A Christian baby shower should honor the birth of a new child. Make it something that would send mothers home to be better mothers. Let the mothers each tell the honoree something that they have learned about children, and in so doing you will help the person who is going to have the child. Also, all the mothers will be helped by one another in what is shared.

What are your goals for a shower? Do you know that unsaved women will come to a church building at the time of a loved one's shower when you couldn't get them there any other time? I don't mean you have to have a preaching service, but you could get up and tell them when the bride was saved. You could tell about when the bride made Jesus master of her life. Use songs that go along with it between the telling of each of these times in her life. You could have someone tell about when she gave her word that she would become the bride to this person she is going to marry. Honor her in this way and help those people to realize the fellowship and the love you have together.

What are your goals? Is your goal just to get together and have a good time? Is it just a social time as the world has it, and you simply dignify it with a prayer so that you can say it is a church time? If you really want to be used of God, this will not do! It just won't do!

Again, what are your goals? Every shower should have as one of its goals to get someone saved! I believe that if the unsaved saw the love they should see in the women of the church, some of them, somewhere, sometime, would come up to a lady and say, "What is this all about?" I've never heard of this happening. I'd just like to know if this has happened. One of the main goals is to honor the person for whom we are having the shower, but let's be sure that someone who is unsaved could get the plan of salvation while they are there in the church building! As we let the Holy Spirit work in our lives, let us make the words of this song our goal: *To be used of God, to sing, to speak, to pray, / To be used of God, to show someone the way, / I long so much to feel the touch of His consuming fire! / To be used of God is my desire.*

To Be Used of God
to Love and Obey Your Husband

Perhaps loving and obeying your husband isn't even your desire. The song is not just "to sing, to speak, to pray"; it is to be used of God to love and obey your husband. Even though you may think you have a better plan than the one your husband has, that is not your privilege to say. You put yourself down, and God will put you up. When you put yourself down, your husband will put you up! It can be a beautiful cycle. You please him and do what he wants you to do, and he will turn around and please you. Instead of having a vicious cycle, as there is in so many marriages, (and, I'm sorry to say, in many Christian marriages), we can have a beautiful cycle where we are working as hard as we can for the good of the other person.

We need to love the other person so much that we want what he wants. Sometimes it will be a like or a want that we do not even understand. It doesn't matter whether or not we understand when we have decided that we are going to please our husbands.

Do you really love your husband? You say, "I have his meals ready. I have his home fixed." Could you have his home fixed in such a way that he doesn't even feel at home in his own home? You could spend lots of time matching the towels. You could spend much time and money on gilding a bird cage and putting plants in it. It could be beautiful, like a picture out of a magazine, but have you ever heard a boy remark, "Mom, I remember that swell bathroom you had back home"?

No, they say, "Mom, I remember how I used to bring my friends in, and we could tromp into the kitchen, raid the refrigerator, sit down, and talk to you. You would listen to us instead of flitting all over."

Why we do these things is what is so important! So many times we keep house and stay home with the children, and we say it is for them. Is it for them? Is it for our husbands? Do we really care that they know that they are really loved? You say, "I'm not very demonstrative!" Then get demonstrative. Start demonstrating that love! Tell God you must show it. You must not just have it; you must show it! This is possi-

Lack of Loving Your Husband and Children

ble if we realize that everything we do can be done not because we have love but because God is love and He is in us!! Because the Lord Jesus is in us, He can do it through us if we simply *"...rejoice in the Lord alway: and again I say, Rejoice!"*

Are You Pushing, Pulling, or Hindering Your Husband?

There are some women who come to Pastors' School with their husbands. Many of these ladies leave with a husband who is also returning home with a new vision! Many times these same wives had wanted their husbands to be more of a leader. Now, all of a sudden, he wants to be more of a leader, and guess who opposes him? His wife—the very wife who had said, "If only my husband were like so-and-so (some great leader she admires)!"

Then, when he gets a little bit of this same type of leadership and wants more, maybe he makes some of the same foolish, stupid mistakes like the adolescent struggling through that 12-, 13-, 14-year-old period when he is becoming an adult. Yes, a man becoming a strong leader might do some stupid things.

And far too often, guess who is there to say, "Isn't that stupid?" YOU! Woman, you are probably going to be the one to decide whether or not that husband is going to go ahead and do exactly what God wants him to do! Do you want a strong leader?

There are so many subtle ways that you can stop your husband. This is for those of you who are married and have children. Perhaps you have said to your daughters, "Honey, let's get two dresses. I know Daddy said just one, but let's get two and put that other one under the bed. We will pull it out when Daddy is in a good mood and tell him about it then." Have you ever tried that one? I can read your minds! I know some of you do it!

THE FIVE SINS OF CHRISTIAN WOMEN

Or have you ever used your husband as an excuse not to serve God? At home when he tells you to do something, you argue with him. You really don't want to please him as you should. You go to church, and when someone asks you to do this or that, you say, "I'll have to ask my husband."

You already know exactly what your husband will want you to do. He hasn't told you to ask him that at all. You *use* him when you do not want to do something. But when it is something that you are supposed to do, you don't or won't obey your husband! Have you ever tried any of these? I'm sure you have!

Mrs. Adoniram (Ann) Judson's life has come through to me in a way that no other woman's life has. She was a full-time Christian worker's wife. Ann Judson lost every bit of her hair while she was on the mission field of Burma with her husband. She had come from a beautiful, lovely home with parents who loved her and who did not want her to go to the mission field. She was someone in society, but she decided, "I'll go. I'll do exactly what my husband feels God wants him to do. I'll be called right along with my husband."

When her husband went to prison, she disguised the manuscript on which he was working for the Burmese people, took it to him in prison, and let him lay on it as if it were a pillow. She was responsible for the fact that 100 years later the Bible is still being read by those people because of the translation that Adoniram Judson made.

Will anyone ever know what Ann Judson did— what a part she had? It will not matter whether or not they do! You know how I found out about Ann Judson? I read a biography entitled *Adoniram Judson: Missionary to Burma*, by Faith Coxe Bailey. Isn't that great? I found out that he could have never been what he was without his wife Ann.

Ann Judson surely went through a kind of humiliation when all of her hair fell out due to a sickness. Ladies, you know

Lack of Loving Your Husband and Children

how hair is so very important! I've heard so many of you say, "I don't care if I don't look right otherwise, but my hair has to be right!" You will do almost anything before you break one of those beauty shop appointments. The only thing Ann Judson had to put over her bald head was an unattractive old cap, and yet she was able to joke with her husband about it!

She could have said, "You have let my health go. You are staying here with the work; please put me first! Take me home. You are doing nothing for me. My health is breaking, and I'm actually dying because I need medicine! I need my family! I need the United States!" Because I know what kind of power women have over men, I have no doubt that Ann Judson could have taken Adoniram home, and he would never have prepared the Burmese Bible, nor an English-Burmese dictionary and grammar.

I'm writing to a wife who will be responsible for her husband's leaving of the will of God. Perhaps he will leave Bible college when he should not. We have had some couples attend Hyles-Anderson College who left prematurely. Now the husband is not in school, not working for the Lord—doing nothing that the Lord has called him to do because his wife could not take it!

Instead of obeying God and her husband, some wife thought, "I've got to have *my* way. I've got to be sure I'm taken care of."

Women, I'm begging with you and pleading with you, we have to be a group of different women! We need some women who will stand out as did Ann Judson. Some will say, "I'm with my husband! Like Ann Judson, I will stand by his side even if it means suffering! I will stand by his side even if it means going to the prison like Ann Judson. She charmed the prison guards so she could get in to see Adoniram and give him nourishing food to keep him alive so he could keep working on that Bible! That kind of courage is what we are going to have to have! We don't have very many women like that!

If I could see every one of you who reads this book and ask, "How many women do you know who could face up to the kind of test Ann Judson passed?" More than likely, most wouldn't be able to hold up one finger! You don't know anyone like Ann! Now think hard. Do you know one woman who could stand this type of test?

Or do you know the kind of woman who constantly gets with others and says, "I just don't know what I'm going to do!" Preachers' wives say, "I don't know why they treat my husband like this. I think he is worthy of more than this. If they fully understood him, they wouldn't treat him like this."

A wife should stay by her husband's side and keep her mouth shut! She should love him and do everything she can to encourage him. She should say, "Go on! It is all right! Don't worry about me!"

The husband often has to worry about the wife and about her feelings because her feelings are uppermost in her life. Oh, that we women could crucify those feelings! We should say, "I am going to die to myself. I am going to live for Christ." Philippians 1:21 says, *For me to live is Christ, and to die is gain.* Women, we've got to learn and apply that verse—not only memorize it—but practice its meaning in our lives and ask God to help us in this matter!

And There Was a Woman in the Church...

"There was a woman in the church." I cannot count how many young pastors have said to me, "I quit the church because there was this woman in the church." Ladies, have you ever known a woman who, by her bitter tongue, can turn her church into a chaos? She can turn a home into a hell.

How much better it is to hear pastors say, "There was this lady in the church who shed joy abroad." I can think of some women like that in a former pastorate that my husband held.

Lack of Loving Your Husband and Children

Anytime we needed anything, those ladies were there. Anytime there was a death or trouble, they were there. They were present on soul-winning nights. They didn't push in, but they were always ready to help when we needed them. And, they were ready to stand back if ever we did not need them. Those women spread joy.

Even though I do not understand football, I attended a game one time with my husband. As I sat watching that Tennessee-Auburn game, I can remember thinking, "This is really something!" Bill Battle, the coach, sent a whole new team out on the field and told the others to came back. When the team returned to the bench, the team members didn't cry or fuss and say, "How come you took me out?" This attitude made me think, "Love is teamwork!" Love gives encouragement and cries, "Go ahead, go ahead, all the way, all the way!" As I watched the game continue, I grabbed my notepad and pen and started writing thoughts. Perhaps you will be a bench warmer for a while! Someone will undoubtedly need that encouragement only you can give! To be sure, all of us are bench warmers at different times, and we should sit there and give out all the strength and love we can in every way. This care should just shine from our eyes.

Ladies, in the same way you should look at your preacher-husbands when they are preaching and show your encouragement. Never give him little signs of what he should say; instead, give him all of the encouragement and love you can give him. Sit and watch him with love in your eyes. If you give him that type of encouragement, there won't be a problem of his not being a man or not having strength.

We don't have men because we don't have ladies! We don't have ladies who, when they are around their husbands, are fulfilling the role which the Bible assigns to them. Fulfilling your proper role is where you find the happiness. When you are a lady, he becomes a man! Glorify his manhood. You can glory in the fact of his becoming stronger and more and more used of God.

Sometimes you have to sit back, and sometimes God will have to put you back. Maybe He will have to put you flat on your back and make you sick for a while so that you will realize what it is to need the husband God has given you! Why should it take that kind of situation?

The Word of God tells wives what to do. Yes, women say, "I obey. I'm not domineering or bossy"; yet, I hear and see otherwise from when they are in public. I hear this from myself sometimes.

Once when our children were younger, our family was stopping by a Kentucky Fried Chicken restaurant. When the children and I were alone, I had stopped there several times, and I would run in and give the order. That particular day, as we were all on our way out of town, we stopped to get fried chicken, and I took over—as normal!

My husband just stood and looked at me in a bewildered way and finally said, "I don't believe it! I cannot believe it!"

Of course, I immediately realized what I had done. I had acted like I was in charge!! I was totally chagrined. In the same way, I think we wives are so used to taking over when we need to do so, that we don't even know when we take over! I guess I think we are all victims of woman's lib whether or not we believe it.

"Do You Want to Please Your Husband in Every Way?"

"I don't domineer. I don't boss my husband," say women; yet neither do they do every little thing that would please him. If he gives you the look with the eyes that says he doesn't want you to do something, it is your pleasure not to do it. If our marriage pictures Christ and the church, then this means that we should want to do every little thing to please our husbands. Is

Lack of Loving Your Husband and Children

this what you want? Do you want to please him in every way? That is the kind of woman we want at Hyles-Anderson College. This is the type of woman God wants in our fundamental churches. If we had these types, we could have some men of God! A man could come home and know that he has a wife waiting who wants his best every minute of the day. If men had wives who wanted only their best, they could endure fighting their own battles.

By the way, wife, you don't have to fight his battles for him. It is such a relief and relaxation for a wife to know and realize that she does not have to fight her husband's battles. All she needs to do is love and encourage him and to let him know that she knows he knows how to fight his own battles.

Wife, relax and ask God to take care of your husband. Let him take care of himself with God's help. It will be so much better for both of you, and it is God's plan. Let's do it with God's grace. It does take God's grace, I know! Desire to have it said about you that "There was a woman in the church who was good. I've never heard her say anything evil about anyone." Ask God to help you to be that kind of woman!

The World's Greatest Home Breakers—Children!

Brother Hyles taught that children were potential home breakers. Sometimes, children can drive a husband and wife apart. The husband and wife can even get to the place that they don't even talk to each other unless a problem arises. "Should we have a new roof on the house?" or "Do the kids need a new pair of shoes?"

You don't know what your husband thinks, what his plans are, or what his thoughts are. You know nothing about his goals. You just do not *know* your husband. How can you please him when you don't know him? Yes, love those children; they are his, but some day those children are going to be gone. When that times come, will you even know your husband?

Many of you make so many excuses.
- "Well, my husband is just not worthy." Look, not one person is worthy of Christ's love.
- "I just can't forget that thing he did once. I'm just not able to forget." Think of your sins and think of things that God has had to forget about you, and then you will be able to forget what he did that time. It is not enough to suppress those feelings. If you suppress those feelings, your stomach will churn, and you'll have ulcers, backaches, neck aches and every other kind of ache. You have to get rid of those feelings! You have to forget those things. Do not think on his past mistakes. Just pray and thank God for him.
- "He's not a leader! If he were some great leader, I could forget!" No, you couldn't! You would not do it then if you can't do it now! If you can't do it when he is just a student in college, when you think he has an unimportant position in fundamentalism, you won't do it later. Or perhaps you say the following about someone else.
- "Oh, if he were only a leader! He could put her in her place and make her the happy woman she is supposed to be." But then as soon as he tries to become a leader, you say, "He is so adolescent about it!" Leaders aren't born overnight.

Want Much for Your Christian Marriage!

A couple should desire to have a marriage based on love and caring. People should not marry to escape loneliness or an unhappy situation, to gain status, or to solve problems. A couple should care about each other as much as each one cares about himself or herself. Set some goals for your marriage.

Decide to always try to cooperate with each other. With give and take, a couple can avoid resentment and anger. By working together, a couple can overcome obstacles. The end result will be satisfaction and gratification.

Decide to have a true partnership. A couple should decide

to be equal in regard to their basic needs, their desires to belong, to be accepted, and to be loved. A marriage partnership can and will succeed if they can maintain this equality.

Decide to develop confidence in yourselves—individually and in each other. A couple can have no room for hatred, envy, jealousy, selfishness, or conceit in marriage. They can have room for leniency, good heartedness, generosity, and tolerance.

Decide to be best friends. A couple needs to have good times to share, to laugh, and to shout. Enough sad times will come. A marriage needs to be flexible enough to allow for the changes together as well as the changes each will experience individually.

Decide to work hard at your marriage. All couples will feel annoyed with one another from time to time. After all, two people will have differences and idiosyncrasies. At times, one will feel his or her needs are not being met entirely. Intend for the marriage to survive the trying periods and to only grow stronger.

Decide to use the intimate marital relationship to be an expression of love—caring, sharing, touching, loving. That relationship alone cannot sustain a faltering marriage nor be the only basis for a new marriage. A couple needs to work on all the avenues that marriage brings into their lives to experience total fulfillment.

Do you really love your husband? Do you really want him to be your leader? Remember, he won't always do what you want him to do anymore. You can't get him to go out and spend a couple of hours visiting with you. Now, you are not sure you want a leader anymore. Do you really want to pay the price? Do you really want someone who is going to be led of God to do a great work for Him? You had better ask yourself that first!

CHAPTER FOUR

Immodest Dress

> "Your clothing reveals your attitude about yourself and authority."
> – Mrs. Beverly Hyles

LET'S TALK ABOUT another one of the sins of Christian women—immodest dress! I go into fundamental churches all the time finding women are dressing with skirts halfway up their thighs. I've gone to Mother-Daughter Banquets, and the women have on their pant suits. The thing I wasn't used to and that broke my heart was the fact that they had a fashion show in front of those unsaved women! Girls modeled dresses halfway up their thighs. Then a fine-looking lady got up and said, "We would have had so-and-so model her halter and shorts, but she didn't get them done," and my heart broke!

I am not talking about a liberal church. This was a fundamental church where the people said they wanted souls saved and that they believed the Bible. When I gave "The Five Sins of Christian Women" as I do the first time I go to a woman's group, I promised God that I would say it all. I was shaking, and my hands were cold that night. I talked weakly and said, "I know you don't agree with me, but I've got to tell you." I wasn't very bold in my presentation, but I told them. I walked out almost by myself.

A few girls did come up to some girls who were with me and said, "That's right. She's right. We know exactly why we are wearing the short dresses." But the mothers didn't come up to me. The kids knew it before their Mamas knew it! That is a pitiful thought.

I have been in a fundamental church where a daily Vacation Bible School program was held to close out the week, and I watched helpers wearing short shorts assist with children on the platform. Unsaved men were sitting in that Vacation Bible School program because their kids had attended all week. How could a man possibly listen? The plan of salvation was given over and over in the program. How could an unsaved man have gotten the plan of salvation?

You say, "Men shouldn't be like that!" Oh, come on, have you ever studied biology? Don't you remember anything? Some of you are married, and you act so pious. What do you mean they shouldn't act like that! Women are the ones who shouldn't act like that! Sure, by God's grace some good Christian men see to it that they keep their eyes off that sort of thing.

This is what my husband says about this kind of incident involving shorts. "At least, when the night club advertises a leg show, they produce the leg show." And he adds, "I have more respect for that night club than I do for a church that advertises a Gospel service and produces a leg show!"

God help us when our fundamental churches are like that! You say, "It doesn't matter; it is what is on the inside." Yes, God looks on the inside, but a man looks on the outside, so it matters so much! I Samuel 16:7 says, *"But the LORD said unto Samuel, Look not on his countenance, or on the height of his stature; because I have refused him: for the LORD seeth not as man seeth; for man looketh on the outward appearance, but the LORD looketh on the heart."* That old line won't stand up at all.

How we dress affects out behavior and our hearts so much! I know you can wear the right clothes and have a wicked heart. I promise you that I know that. Don't let that argument be an excuse for you. That kind of justification doesn't give you a license for anything! You can say, "We aren't under law!" I know that also, so because of love and because of grace, let's dress right! We need to realize what we are doing and what we are saying.

What Are the Main Points of Concern for Christian Women's and Girls' Dress?

It seems so many of our problems in life come from the word "too." We talk too much, too little, or too late. We eat too much or too little as in anorexia nervosa. I have the

"Perfect Seven" of dress that all deals with "too." How these "too's" are decided and enforced for you is the important thing. There are ways to make rules for these "too's," and there are ways to measure them and enforce them for yourself, your children, your church youth group activities, or your Christian school.

"The Perfect Seven"
Not too low
Not too tight
Not too short
Not too dowdy
Not too extreme
Not too mannish
Not too sheer or bare

There are several issues concerning Christian ladies and their clothing. Modesty and femininity are just two of the issues. Association with certain groups of the world is a third. Not being too extreme would have caused most ladies during the "hippie" era of the 1960's to refrain from maxi-dresses, although they were perfectly feminine and modest. At that time, they were practically the uniform of rebels who fought the establishment.

Too mannish is, of course, (not even taking pants of any kind into consideration) gauchos and split skirts that pull across the body as pants do. They are not "too mannish." They **are** mannish. "Too mannish" would also be referring to materials, patterns, and styles of suits and dresses that could be easily made into men's clothing. Some of our ladies love to be identified with clothes as tailored and as mannish as possible. They delight in a whole wardrobe of rough-textured material of tweed and stripes to be worn with heavy shoes and boots which appear masculine. It's difficult to understand because everyone knows, "Vivé la différence!"

Being too dowdy actually causes undue attention to be

drawn to a person. Modest, attractive, pretty, colorful, feminine clothing is designed to draw attention to the spirit-filled woman's very spirit, soul, and character which lasts for time and eternity.

Dress so as not to be party to a man's committing adultery **with** you in his heart. *"But I say unto you, That whosoever looketh on a woman to lust after her hath committed adultery with her already in his heart."* (Matthew 5:28)

"Skorts," Split Skirts, Gauchos, Walking Shorts and Trousers by Any Other Name

You who wear pants and are going to do so no matter what, need read no further. You who feel you do not wear pants will want to be sure the Devil is not tricking you. I feel that many of us have been guilty of wearing pants by another name and have felt we were dressed according to what we believe the Bible teaches. Because the world calls whatever it designs other than shorts or skirts "culottes,'" we find most anything at youth activities, women's retreats and picnics—all under the guise of "culottes."

Some of these split-skirt type garments pull across the backside every bit as badly as trousers do, often revealing lines of undergarments in either a very repulsive or sexual way, depending on the person's figure. Once I was sitting behind a lady unable to keep from wondering if that nice person had any idea how she looked from the back when she stood to participate in the singing at a women's meeting. The garment was long enough and full enough in the front, but had so little material in the back that the "full figure" could not be accommodated and was straining at the seams with the hem hiked up to show three inches of fat, veined flesh above the knee. And that, all in the name of dressing to please the Lord.

Since it has been well nigh to impossible to purchase culottes or culotte patterns that look like a skirt in the front and in the back, *Christian Womanhood* has spent hundreds and hundreds of dollars and hours and hours of time developing plans for culottes that cannot be readily recognized as being culottes but rather look like a skirt when a lady or girl is standing, walking, or appropriately active!

No Christian lady has to be a slave to the world's ideas. At times, the world markets dressy, feminine "culottes" with jackets, but you had better check whether or not the back matches the front! No, those pretty culotte sets are pants in the back and not what we think of as culottes at all. Let's be sure the Devil does not succeed in tricking us into thinking we aren't wearing trousers when we really are.

During the summertime especially, there is a problem with see-in and see-through blouses and dresses. Anyone who pays the price to be modest—checking armholes, heights of necklines, sheerness, or how the clothing clings will be considered stupid. When my daughter Joy was a teenager, she and I shopped at an area store. We were told that certain dresses were not too form fitting, low necked or too short. The clerk went on to inform us that "everyone" was wearing them! I had been really nice to her and continued to keep a calm voice as I said, "Just bring us the dresses. We'll check them and decide. We don't wear what everyone else is wearing, but I am sure that we'll find something from all that you have here."

Mothers, You Decide!

Mothers, you can decide what your child is going to wear. You don't have to give in under that pressure, "Everyone's doing it!" Yes, everyone else is also having abortions; everyone else is also walking down the aisle as an impure girl. Sure, they are all doing it. So don't be surprised when a teenage daughter comes home who has had relations with a boy she has been dating, is now having a baby, and is in trouble. Don't be shocked or surprised! When you allow them to dress as they please, **you** are sending them out for that! You are sending them out to seduce instead of talking to them and helping them to know that **after marriage** sex is beautiful and wonderful. **After marriage** is when the seducing should take place, and in the marriage bedroom.

Some girls have been seducing since they were 12 years old, and by the time they are married, they have given it up. That is one reason why we don't have happy marriages. The Bible teaches us to be as discreet as any woman of the Bible ever thought of being **outside** the home, but **inside** the home with her husband, she should be as seductive as any woman could ever be. Somehow, we have gotten it all mixed up! If we do talk about sex, we talk about it in all forms—before and after marriage. That is not what the Bible teaches at all. We have the matter all mixed up!!

I have had women say, "Let's talk about love, joy, the rainbow, the colors of the rainbow, and how women are sweet." I promise you, if I knew some sweet women, I would talk about that!! But I am not one, and I don't know any others. As far as I know, we are all depraved! We sit around in our little ladies' circles and talk about how bad a woman of the street is. When we finish crucifying her, we then talk about how bad the dope head is. We far too easily ignore the very fact that we have our sins in our own camp! We had better take care of that first!

But you say, "Those sweet little girls don't know…they don't understand…they are not thinking about…." That's not what they tell me! The "sweet little girls" tell me they know exactly what they are doing when they wear their dresses halfway up their thigh and bend over the water fountain to take a drink of water. They tell me they know exactly what they are doing!

You see, we are living in a different world than what some of us lived in at their age. They know what is happening! They plan this! They plan that they will sell themselves to the guys around the school with their body. Therefore, the first time a girl comes along with nice legs, she's popular until another girl comes along with better legs, and then she has lost the game! Such girls haven't realized that they must be better girls spiritually and mentally to become all God would have them to be in every facet and phase of their lives. They haven't worked on developing the mental and spiritual part of their lives because some of you have equipped them to seduce! They have realized the power that a female body has, and that is exactly where they have stopped. Now I admit, some do not know, but many of them do know!

Where Are You Getting Your Standards?

I John 2:15–17 says, *"Love not the world, neither the things that are in the world. If any man love the world, the love of the Father is not in him. For all that is in the world, the lust of the flesh, and the lust of the eyes, and the pride of life, is not of the Father, but is of the world. And the world passeth away, and the lust thereof: but he that doeth the will of God abideth for ever."*

Why don't Christians go as far away from the world as possible? I get a little angry—not at people—but at the situation. For instance, the world has to be told that cigarettes are not good for them. We knew that years and years ago from the old-fashioned, fundamental preachers, and yet the world doesn't believe it until the Surgeon General says it!

The world continues on in their confusion. Now the world is saying that any drinking can hurt person, but if you do drink, "don't drive." The thinking is that quite possibly, if a person drinks a couple of bottles of an alcoholic beverage, his reflexes might be diminished; so don't drive. They **know** not to do that! How sorry I feel for the world.

The world system also says that what was fine for safe sex is no longer safe. Seemingly, the world lets the media decide for them exactly what is bad or good for them.

The reason I laugh is because Christians seem to need to have the world's view on a subject before really knowing what the Bible has been saying for almost 100 years. A recent *Parade* magazine said, "This (the *Parade*) has to be the place to get the truth now." How pitiful! The *Parade* is now masquerading as the world's authority.

Whether or not it is the authority doesn't matter. Let me share what I read in a *Parade* magazine. A group of young men were asked by the *Parade* editors, "Does a woman's immodesty provoke rape?" Every one of those men answered "Yes!" In this day of woman's liberation, worldly women would hoot down the answer. I find it interesting that men who are not Christians are somewhat taking a stand more courageous than some of our Christians are.

Let's not be intimidated by the world's people. Biblical thinking is right, and the Bible is right. It's time Christians took responsibility for their actions. Yes, in this day of liberation when we fundamentalists are hooted at for even suggesting that immodest dress should be blamed as a factor for the increase of rape, let's take a stand.

The *Parade* magazine printed better answers to the question of "Does immodest dress provoke rape?" than I have seen in most Christian publications in recent years. We are scared that if we say that it *might* be the dress, that we are condoning the behavior of men who commit the crime of rape. No! We are not! No matter how provocative a woman might dress, the man who commits that horrible crime should pay. But that is not what I am addressing at all. I am saying that, if a horrible thing like rape were to happen to you or one of yours, you would certainly feel a lot better about the situation if you knew beyond a shadow of a doubt that you had done nothing to provoke the attack. Not one item of clothing you were wearing could have caused the provocation.

People, be logical. Just think about what the Bible says. Most men seeing a woman in a skimpy bathing suit or garment too tight would have a difficult time following Matthew 5:27 and 28. *"Ye have heard that it was said by them of old time, Thou shalt not commit adultery: But I say unto you, That whosoever looketh on a woman to lust after her hath committed adultery with her already in his heart."* Surely you would not want to be a part of adultery of the mind because of the provocation in your dress or the way you walk, sit, or stand! Even a little logic left in the world today can resign to the fact that problems progress from small to large.

The world can still logic it out. Yes, according to "worldly" men, a woman's dress can provoke a man to commit the unthinkable crime of rape. Some people have still retained enough common sense to recognize "Oh, be careful little eyes what you see." I wonder if we need a song for adults that says, "Oh, be careful big eyes what you see."

Proverbs 7:10 says, *"And, behold, there met him a woman with the attire of an harlot, and subtil of heart."* It surely seems to me that we need to decide what the attire of a harlot is and stay as far away from it as possible! We've spent so much time looking down our noses at the women of the street that we really do not understand that we commit this sin.

You Are a Walking Advertisement!

If you are reading this book with an open mind and asking the Holy Spirit to help you understand, I believe you have the excellent spirit that characterized Daniel. *"Then this Daniel was preferred above the presidents and princes, because an excellent spirit was in him; and the king thought to set him over the whole realm."* (Daniel 6:3) I just want you to try to take in what we teach about dress and say, "Please, Lord; help me to be open to Your will in the area of my dress."

I am fortunate to be a part of an organization that sets a

standard and enforces it. Rules were not made in order to have rules. You might say, "No one else goes by your rules, especially not the world." Well, let's face it; the world isn't doing very well right now. So it does not really matter what the world does. The question is whether or not we want to be different and whether or not you want to have an influence and be used by God. I Corinthians 10:31says, *"Whether therefore ye eat, or drink, or whatsoever ye do, do all to the glory of God."*

Certainly, we would want to wear clothes that would glorify God. Also, we would want to go by the Word of God. Let's read again Proverbs 7:10, which says, *"And, behold, there met him a woman with the attire of an harlot, and subtil of heart."*

That Scripture teaches that there is an attire of a woman of the street. Most of us have heard and think we understand or know that this verse is speaking of a slit above the knee—whether or not it was a short skirt, a long skirt, or a slinky skirt. We would surely want to be as far away from that kind of attire as possible. Look at yourself in the mirror and ask yourself, "Would this dress be pleasing to Jesus?" I Thessalonians 2:4b says, *"Not as pleasing men, but God, which trieth our hearts."* I hope some of you will make these your own standards for the sake of your influence.

Maybe, you have had a good heart without doing anything about what I have been teaching about women's dress. Let me say that the way a lady dresses has nothing to do with going to Heaven. The blood of Jesus Christ gets us to Heaven. If you die in a pair of pants, you will still get to go to Heaven? This issue has nothing to do with that.

This issue has something to do with influence. Your influence could help other people go to Heaven. Your influence might help young girls become feminine young ladies. Yes, God does look on the heart, and if you have a good heart, He sees that heart no matter what you are wearing. However, I Samuel 16:7 says, *"Man looketh on the outward appearance..."* Man

Immodest Dress

does look on the outward appearance, and there are so many times wonderful ladies are not aware of their appearance. Some do not even know they are being immodest, and they would not even think of showing themselves. The problem is that these good ladies are not looking in the mirror to enforce those rules that would keep them modest.

At Hyles-Anderson College, the standards and rules we follow were devised by men of God. Those standards and rules are adopted by those who attend this college. We, who work at the college, enforce these rules. We want the men in our college to not have a single lustful thought. It makes me so happy to know that there is an organization that is trying to keep its girls modest.

I am asking you to look at yourself every time you go by a mirror and ask yourself, "Am I pleasing the Lord with my dress?" I am also asking you, **for the sake of your influence,** to make these standards of dress your standards of dress. I can promise you that you will be viewed as feminine.

She's Feminine! She's Different!

One time when I was at Mayo Clinic, I watched girls come and go from that 18-floor building. I would see guys watch them and give that "knowing look." I understand that about 4,000 people go through the doors of Mayo Clinic every week.

Time after time, I couldn't help but notice a certain girl come to one of the desks. She had on a crepe dress of soft, feminine material with a ruffle around the bottom of her knee-length dress. She had pearls around her neck. She was not a beautiful girl. Her hair was fairly long with a feminine style. I saw men watching her, and there was a different look on their faces when they looked at her than when they had looked at the other girls. There was what I call a look of devotion and worship in the eyes of those men!

I watched that girl and decided she must be from a Christian college. (However, not all girls dress that way when they are away from their Christian college, I'm sorry to say!) One day I asked her, "Do you attend a Christian college?"

"Yes," she said. "I'm from Bob Jones University."

I said, "Praise the Lord!" I sat down and promptly wrote a letter to the leaders at Bob Jones University and told them, "Thank you! Your girl stood out!"

Not all of them do because some decide they won't pay the price! I thought, "Oh, I want the girls from Hyles-Anderson College to be the type of girls whom guys could be around and say, "Thank You, God, for this lady!" Men **do** want to be around feminine loveliness that will bring out their best in manliness!

I wish every one of us could look our very best for the Lord Jesus! We are not talking about looking dowdy and ugly. We are talking about looking lovely, the way Proverbs 31 talks about the woman with her tapestry and purple. There is a kind of loveliness in a girl or a woman that gives her the title of "lady," and men want to be gentlemen when they are around her. That is the kind of girls and women I want you to be! If that is the kind of lady you want to be, you are going to have to be different from the whole wide world!

Certainly, many of us have at one time or another salved our consciences with old but untrue remarks such as, "You can be a good Christian and wear trousers!" I am not talking about what you can do and still be a Christian. "My legs just get so cold that I have to wear trousers." "I am required to wear trousers at my job." "I'm in sports, and it is more modest to wear trousers." Men don't understand this reasoning, but I agree that it is fun to sit around wearing trousers; it is more relaxed. Some girls who have worn trousers all of their lives do not know how to sit, walk, or stand in a dress! Please let me remind you that there is more than a modesty issue on this subject. There is the issue of dressing as a lady at all times.

We have had girls attend Hyles-Anderson College who took the heel of their right foot and put it up on the left knee when they sat down—when they were wearing a dress! They sat with their legs all sprawled out! They have been cheated out of learning how to look like a girl. They found out they had wanted to look and feel like a lady for years and hadn't found anyone they wanted to copy.

There's a Price to Pay!

Women, we are talking about something so far above the ordinary. If you are called to be a different woman, you will stand out! There is a price to pay! Let me tell you about our preacher's wife, Mrs. Jack Hyles. She is beautiful and lovely. If I ever saw her in a pair of pants, I'd just die, and women who wear pants would too. They would be disappointed because, you see, she is a princess, she is a queen, she is a lady, she is special! Little girls adore her. Teenagers admire her. Ladies in her age group look to her as their heroine. Older ladies highly respect her. Men treat her as a lady of ladies. Could it be that she is always a lady?

Now please don't take the attitude, "I'm *somebody* if I don't wear trousers!" No, you are nobody if you take that kind of attitude. Say, "By the grace of God, I'm going to be different, not because I'm anything, but because God called me to be different. He is making me different." If that is what you truly want, you will stand out as our preacher's wife stands out.

I've had a wonderful heritage. I have been blessed doubly with another model preacher's wife, Mrs. Lee Roberson. For 11 years, I never saw her dress anyway but right. She was a standard setter, an example—someone to whom the ladies of the church could look.

We are not talking about just being a cute girl. Do you know, I think girls are cute in pant suits? I have seen some pant suits that I think are really cute. I think some little, slender girls are darling in them, but "cute girls" never change the world. It has always been the Queen Elizabeths, the Ann Judsons, the Susanna Wesleys, the Betty Stams, the Susannah Spurgeons, the Caroline Robersons, the Beverly Hyleses—ladies with a purpose greater than themselves. God help us to be somebody different.

You say, "I don't believe that stuff about pants that you all talk about." I know some verses that I could show you, but let's not even talk about the Bible. Now that is funny for me to say, isn't it? I know all of the arguments; I've heard them all. Instead, let me ask these questions:

- **Do I want to wear clothes that help me look as different from a man as possible?** What garment is as different as possible from those most men wear?" Of course, a skirt or a dress!

- **Do I want to learn to walk, sit, and stand as differently from a man as possible?** Can I learn that best wearing a skirt or trousers? If you don't have the vision to be a lady, let's say a model. Did you know that charm schools and modeling schools teach their students to stay out of trousers? They have learned that a model will walk, sit, and stand incorrectly if she wears pants! Models will give up their trousers in order to sell clothes. Will Christian girls and women pay the price to dress modestly and look their best to serve the Lord?

- **Do I want every line of my undergarments or body to show?** What type of clothing most helps to eliminate this problem—a well-fitting skirt or trousers? If you will be truthful, you know that when you wear pants, every move of your body shows. I don't care if the pants are tight or if they are loose, every movement of your body shows. There is a freedom in wearing trousers that reflects masculine traits that a lady should not have. You say, "There are some sports I like to play, and I need to wear pants."

Well, the late Mrs. John R. Rice got along without pants, and she rode horses! Her sister-in-law, Dr. Cathy Rice, gets along just fine without wearing pants, and she rides horses, too! If we carry ourselves in a ladylike manner and avoid work or activities that are totally unladylike, we are not going to be in much trouble in any activity which cannot be performed in well-made culottes—that look like a skirt in the front and in the back.

If we are truly cold, we can wear leotards or tights under a sporty skirt, fashion boots, leg warmers, maxi-skirts, and anything we set our minds to invent. We women are very creative and adaptable if we choose to be. What little inconveniences we cannot avoid will be well repaid in the feeling we get from doing right and dressing as a lady. People make beautiful, encouraging remarks about a real lady—even the unsaved notice!

It's surprising how few employers we have found who will not help girls around the "pants-only" rule. Generally speaking, employers are not the problem; we are. Let's be pretty and as feminine as it's within our power to be. God will help us to be happy because we're modest and ladylike.

I believe you can find a way if you want to find one. You can find arguments if you don't want to go along with it. Don't argue over it! Just be what you want to be and do what you think is right for you, but I'd talk to the Lord a lot about it. Sure, you can be a Christian, but do you want to be different? Do you want to be a different woman?

Here Come "the Skirts"!

A waitress at the local Cracker Barrel Restaurant once told me that she and others of our church members who work at that restaurant are usually called upon to serve the tables occupied by "the skirts" who eat at that restaurant. I was afraid I immediately knew what she meant but asked her to tell me about it. She said that when waitresses see a group of ladies all coming in skirts and dresses, they know they won't get a good tip from them. I don't know if this is true. I hope it's not true, but at least the people in that restaurant think that ladies dressed modestly with femininity do not tip as well as other people.

My mind immediately went back to the time I was in chapel listening to my college dean saying, "You people who don't have enough money to tip don't have enough money to go out to eat at this Howard Johnson's over here on the corner." At that time, Howard Johnson's was a very nice restaurant, at least in that city, and we all loved going to such a nice, new, attractive place.

I know that some of you do not like the custom of tipping in a restaurant, but it is something that seems to have to be lived with whether or not we like it. Time after time polls have been taken by advice columnists and all manner of restaurant associations to see if the general public would rather pay more for their meals so that waitresses and waiters could get a decent wage without tips. All polls seem to come back with the consensus that people want to have the chance to reward their server according to the service given.

There are a lot of books and articles written on proper tipping, and I do not know that I am one who understands all that they say. I have chosen to tip 20 percent of the bill in fine dining situations with no less than 15 percent given in any other type of eating place. If I stay at a booth or table in a working luncheon way longer than the usual dining time, I try to tip as if I were a second customer. There are those around me who say that the table would not have been in use anyway as they see an empty building, but our staying at a table keeps a good server concerned about whether or not the needs of the guests are being met.

Let's let "the skirts" stand for kindness and thoughtfulness as we realize that good restaurant servers give all that they have mentally, physically, emotionally, and socially to do their job well. Perhaps it would be better to order less in order to have proper tipping money.

In thinking about this one issue of tipping, I began to wonder what else "the skirts" stand for. I wonder if they stand for gossip? Talk against their husbands? Complaining? Criticism of their church? I think we would be surprised to know how much servers overhear when we are engrossed in our conversation as they come in and out of the situation. If we don't tip right and we don't talk right, we probably had better not leave a tract with our church's name on it! Why would they want to have anything we have?

I hope servers come running to try to get you at one of their tables when someone says, "Here come 'the skirts'."

CHAPTER FIVE

Lack of Soul Winning, Bible, and Prayer

> "If there is a Hell with real fire where unsaved people go, then I say that a person who does not warn people about it does not have real love."
> –Dr. Jack Hyles

T̲HE SIN I discuss last in this book is probably first in importance because it will help us with every other sin.

Reproduction is one of the greatest needs in the life of every living person. God made us this way and, of course, understands the need and, as always, makes a way to meet the need. A loving, heavenly Father planned for our happiness through Matthew 28:19, 20, which says, *"Go ye therefore, and teach all nations, baptizing them in the name of the Father, and of the Son, and of the Holy Ghost: Teaching them to observe all things whatsoever I have commanded you: and, lo, I am with you alway, even unto the end of the world. Amen."* He could have left it entirely to the Holy Spirit, but He didn't. He gave us a part, a very big part; that of soul winner!

Spiritual reproduction through leading souls to Christ and then teaching them can go on for our entire lifetime. There is no such thing as "over the hill" in this kind of reproduction. There is no cause for "empty-nest syndrome" outside of our own stubbornness, laziness, and lack of willingness to learn. People of every background, temperament, or position can be soul winners and teachers of good things. The people who are most shy are oftentimes the most effective soul winners as they have to depend on God instead of a dynamic personality.

He would have specified what type of people couldn't get in on Matthew 28:19, 20 if He hadn't planned to hold everyone accountable. More importantly, He planned to make the rewards open for everyone to gain: no one is eliminated! *"The fruit of the righteous is a tree of life; and he that winneth souls is wise."* (Proverbs 11:30) *"And they that be wise shall shine as the brightness of the firmament; and they that turn many to righteousness as the stars for ever and ever."* (Daniel 12:3)

I once had a rather wealthy lady tell me, "We used to go on visitation but don't get to do that anymore. We feel our part is giving so the work can go on." She all but told me they could pay their way out of their soul-winning obligations. The tragic thing about that attitude is the natural decay that sets in when spiritual reproduction stops. In the case I have just mentioned, it did set in—and soon, much to my sorrow.

God also gives us fun and excitement through our soul-winning experiences. Soul winning is where we get our excitement! I dare say you have not seen many real soul winners backslide! Christianity is not really that exciting when you are not doing what God planned for you to do! Don't you believe that He could win souls without us? Don't you believe He could do it all? God usually chooses to use three parts:

1. There is the part of the soul winner
2. There is the part of the one being won
3. There is the Holy Spirit's part.

Why did God choose to use human beings when we are so weak? I wonder if He didn't do it for our own good. He knows we have to have excitement, and I believe soul winning provides that excitement!

When we moved from Tennessee to Indiana, two men helped move our belongings in a Mayflower van. We said, "When you get to Hammond, it will be Saturday. Stay and go with us to the world's largest church on Sunday."

"If we are not drunk," one of the men replied, "we will."

"Please don't go drinking this weekend," we countered. They didn't! Those two guys, about 25 years of age, stayed with us, slapped up bed frames, made sandwiches, and took baths in cold water. That's right! Certain utilities had not yet been cared for. Not only did they take baths in cold water, but they also used a "blue cow" for soap. In all of the packing, I had lost all of the soap other than an Avon blue cow made to hang from a child's neck!

The men went to church with us and found 35 things wrong with the church. You know how it is when you have vis-

Lack of Soul Winning, Bible, and Prayer

itors. They felt led to tell us there were 35 things that they did not like about the church! They stayed for the evening service, and guess what? They also felt led to tell us everything they didn't like about that service that night! Still, they kept coming back to visit. John, one of the drivers, kept returning every time he made a run into Indianapolis, the Mayflower headquarters. It wasn't for a free meal or a free bed either. Sometimes they would just come in for two or three hours, and my husband would deal with them and stay up into the morning hours. Do you know they would listen and listen, but they just wouldn't get saved!

Now about the third time that Mayflower truck pulled up, our neighbors thought we were schizophrenics. Every time they turned around, a Mayflower moving truck was in front of our house! They'd think (and were hoping) we were moving again! But we didn't! Our kids were the only kids in the neighborhood who got to go for rides in that Mayflower truck!

Besides that, my husband was given the opportunity to drive their Mayflower. He wanted to be a truck driver when he was a little kid, and how he did love driving that Mayflower! With John in the co-captain's seat, he drove over to Baptist City where our college students were, but there was no audience. No one, literally no one, had returned from his Sunday bus route. How disappointing! It's sorta like, "Look, Mom! No hands!" with no Mom to applaud.

If you are a soul winner, people won't be saying, "Those poor little Evans kids," or "Those poor little Christian kids; they don't get to do anything." Our kids were always doing things that other kids wished that they could do. When you are a soul winner, it is exciting! Something is happening all of the time! I can promise you that more goes on at our house than goes on at all the houses of unsaved people around us!

The third time John came, my husband asked, "Why do you keep coming back?"

He said, "I feel like you love me."

The fourth time, he came late one Saturday night. Usually he didn't come on Saturday because he knew he would have to go to church on Sunday. That Sunday morning, the minute Dr. Hyles gave the invitation at our church, he hit the altar. About a year after we moved to Schererville, Indiana, our Mayflower driver was saved!

That afternoon, my husband gave him a list of churches he could attend all over the country—wherever his Mayflower would pull in. He wanted to know everything; whereas before, he hadn't wanted to learn anything. Talk about excitement! Talk about living a life that is full and rich! Only a soul winner could have that kind of life!

"I Feel Sorry for You Ladies Who Do Not Win Souls!"

You know, I really feel sorry for you ladies who do not win souls. You say, "Well, I've tried. I've tried and tried, and all I get are doors slammed in my face."

Let me tell you about one of my friends who is a lovely former model. Do you know who won her to the Lord? An 86-year-old blind lady won her to the Lord over the telephone! I'll be honest with you. If I were God, I would say, "Now there is that former Marshall Fields model; I want her to be saved. I'm going to find a sharp, cute girl to witness to her." God sent an 86-year-old blind lady. God is the One Who does it! It is the Holy Spirit Who does it, but He does it through us. If we will go ahead and do what God tells us to do all the time, He will take care of us. He will be responsible for the souls being won.

Mrs. Fay Dodson first started the Phoster Club in this area. Now God has used her to start Phoster Clubs all over the nation. She has trained hundreds and thousands of women to go out and win souls. We can learn from her or one of her trainees.

Lack of Soul Winning, Bible, and Prayer

Maybe you've gone forward when the Preacher has given an invitation to win souls, but you haven't really done what you promised. Find someone who does win souls and say, "I am going to stay with you until I know how to win souls."

One day, I was with Mrs. Alma Cowling sightseeing on the Mississippi River. I thought I was talking to her. The next thing I knew she was in back of a tavern leading the tavern owner's three children to the Lord! We have since gone back to that church in Illinois, and there are still people in that church who she won that Saturday on the Mississippi River.

She said, "Marlene, I used to be so fearful. I had such an inferiority complex that I couldn't look a person in the eye. About nine years ago I came to the First Baptist Church and learned how to win people to the Lord, and now it is a different story!" She has the boldness of the Holy Spirit. She can go up to a group of six would-be hoodlums, take over the conversation, tell them about Jesus, and they absolutely love her. Yet, she is not the kind of person who can sit around and socialize. Isn't it great to be bold at soul winning and timid about sitting around socializing? Oh, by the way, when you are timid about sitting around socializing, you probably won't be gossiping. Oh, God; please give us more Alma Cowlings!

Now, women, you are going to have to quit the country clubs where you are going golfing. You are going to have to quit it. I don't say there won't be a time when you may go play golf. Some of you are nervous, and the doctor says, "Take up something." And you said, "Well, I guess it will be golf."

Give Up Your Garden Clubs and Cultivate for Eternity!

Some of you are going to have to give up garden clubs. The United States is full of garden clubs, and there are plenty of women to take care of the garden clubs. Now, there is not a thing wrong with garden clubs, unless the club includes gossip, contention, and trouble, but you can expect that in any woman's club! (I'm sorry, but you do!) There are nice things that a garden club can do, but the church is sending you out to plant the seed, win people to Christ, plant them, water them. You've got all the "garden club" you can handle right in your own local church.

Some of you are spending so much of your life in anything other than spiritual. Here is the question, ladies: Is it for time, or is it for time and eternity? Every time you do something, ask yourself that. If it is just for time (garden clubs are just for time)? Do you want to invest your life that way? There might be a time when you need to go out and play golf or work in your garden, but do it just when you need to, so you can go back out and work for the Lord.

Ladies, we are talking about something completely different than what the world has seen! We are not talking about being powerful and great and going down in the history books. Would you like to be used as Susanna Wesley was used? Would you like to be used as Coystal Hyles has been by mothering a son who has done the work that Jack Hyles has done? That is the kind of women about whom we are talking. If you are going to be that kind of woman, you are going to have to pay a price. The price may be the giving up of carrying on with other women—that which you think is fellowship. Usually, it isn't fellowship at all; it's what I call "gossipship!"

Some Soul-Winning Pointers

1. *"He that winneth souls is wise"* whether or not those souls get into church on **your or your friend's timetable.** *"And they that be wise shall shine as the brightness of the firmament; and they that turn many to righteousness as the stars for ever and ever."* (Daniel 12:3)

2. If the souls you won truly believed God raised Jesus from the dead, they are going to meet you in Heaven—

whether or not they ever meet you in church. *"That if thou shalt confess with thy mouth the Lord Jesus, and shalt believe in thine heart that God hath raised him from the dead, thou shalt be saved. For with the heart man believeth unto righteousness: and with the mouth confession is made unto salvation."* (Romans 10:9, 10)

3. Do your best in dealing with the souls you win, but relax in the Holy Spirit as you realize the results are up to Him. *"But ye shall receive power, after that the Holy Ghost is come upon you: and ye shall be witnesses unto me both in Jerusalem, and in all Judæa, and in Samaria, and unto the uttermost part of the earth."* (Acts 1:8)

4. Giving the message is your part, but the convert and the Holy Spirit together have the greater part. This knowledge can keep you humble as you have good results, as well as encourage you when you are not having the results you want.

5. Remember that the world, the flesh, and the Devil will be fighting you all the way (and your Christian friends are also subject to these three). They will be for your decorating, having banquets, preparing music, sending out letters, studying a Sunday school lesson, going to special meetings, and even participating in a Bible study before they will be for soul winning, which is God's heartbeat through the entire Bible. If you can be stopped from winning souls because you cannot show your results at the church, the Devil will have scored a victory.

Let's Start Over!

Decide now that you are going to start winning souls, **and** you want to be able to fulfill the last part of Matthew 28:19 and 20 also. *"Go ye therefore, and teach all nations, baptizing them in the name of the Father, and of the Son, and of the Holy Ghost: Teaching them to observe all things whatsoever I have commanded you: and, lo, I am with you alway, even unto the end of the world. Amen."*

1. After you win someone to Christ, start over just as in starting over in this book. Perhaps we would see better results.

2. After you have won 100 people to Christ, you will see people in church as a result of your soul winning. Keep winning them. I often bump into a lady Sunday school teacher and her entire family who have been in First Baptist Church quietly serving the Lord for 20 years. My husband led the lady to Christ, and I know the scores of families he has led to Christ whom he visits every once in a while but has never seen come to church.

3. See if the convert will go soul winning with you even if he does not want to attend church.

4. Send a note to everyone you win to Christ with all kinds of information as to how they could track you down if they ever need you. They may start to attend church ten years after they trusted Christ for salvation.

5. Keep a list of converts and send the names to people who will pray for them all the rest of their lives.

6. Be assured that people you are least likely to think about are being cared for by the Holy Spirit.

On Which Side of Caution Are You?

I have been asked, "Shouldn't a person be cautious in leading someone to Christ too soon after knowing the person?" Everyone is cautious in one way or another in soul winning.

- One person wants to be sure she doesn't lead someone to accept Christ as Saviour who doesn't completely understand.
- Another person wants to be cautious that she doesn't discourage anyone who might be serious whether or not the person acts a certain way or says the right things. She wants to be cautious that she gives a person the opportunity to accept Christ at a time which might be her last opportunity.

Ever since I first got around people who talked Bible

Lack of Soul Winning, Bible, and Prayer

talk (being saved, winning souls, Heaven and Hell), I have gotten the idea that folks must be given the opportunity to accept Jesus as Saviour immediately upon hearing the Gospel. In 1950 when I was 16 years old, Dr. John R. Rice, Dr. Bill Rice, Brother Joe Rice, Dr. Bob Jones, Sr., Brother Joe Henry Hankins and others were the ones who gave me the idea at a one-week Sword conference in Siloam Springs, Arkansas. They said there were people they had known whom they had not told about Jesus who had died and gone to Hell as far as they knew. I thought that was pretty horrible.

I had also been led to believe by the radio program, "The Old-Fashioned Revival Hour," led by Dr. Charles E. Fuller, that people should be told to come to Christ as soon as the Holy Spirit put you into contact with them. At least, I can still remember Dr. Fuller saying, "Come sailors, come soldiers, give your hearts to Jesus before you ship out. You, in the balcony, come on down, son." This was sometime during World War II, 1941–1946, and I was born in 1933, so I was fairly young when I got the idea that, *"For whosoever shall call upon the name of the Lord shall be saved."* (Romans 10:13) I didn't think Dr. Fuller knew those guys in that Long Beach, California, Municipal Auditorium. I didn't think he'd ever get to know them because those guys were leaving right away to go to the Pacific to fight.

To my shame, I'm not trying to imply that I've been able to say, *"For we cannot but speak the things which we have seen and heard."* (Acts 4:20) But, I do say I have no excuse for I've known by implication from radio messages, if nothing else, from early on that, *"Neither is there salvation in any other: for there is none other name under heaven given among men, whereby we must be saved."* (Acts 4:12)

Acts 4:13 assures me that I don't have to be smart to have the boldness to tell about Jesus if Peter and John were not considered smart. *"Now when they saw the boldness of Peter and John, and perceived that they were unlearned and ignorant men, they marvelled; and they took knowledge of them, that they had been with Jesus."* All I have to do is stay with Jesus then.

Now in more recent years, I've recognized that I'm just the human instrument God uses to get His message of salvation to people. The Holy Spirit has a part, the person hearing has a part, and I have a part. Probably I'm the least of the three parts in getting a person saved. I'm just happy we as individuals have any part. I know I need to be needed by God, and He made His plan of witness to include me. *"But ye shall receive power, after that the Holy Ghost is come upon you: and ye shall be witnesses unto me both in Jerusalem, and in all Judæa, and in Samaria, and unto the uttermost part of the earth."* (Acts 1:8)

He could have called 10,000 angels to win souls, but He chose to use Christians. *"Go ye therefore, and teach all nations, baptizing them in the name of the Father, and of the Son, and of the Holy Ghost: Teaching them to observe all things whatsoever I have commanded you: and, lo, I am with you alway, even unto the end of the world. Amen."* (Matthew 28:19, 20)

Logically, then, from the Word of God and from God's men who preach that Word, I have come to the conclusion that I'm to try to lead everyone with whom the Holy Spirit gives me contact to a saving knowledge of Jesus Christ. I may very well be the last Christian he knows before he goes into eternity. Now that I am over 60 years old, I have known of that to happen over and over.

Logically, I see that I'm supposed to help every newborn Christian to grow in grace. *"Then they that gladly received his word were baptized: and the same day there were added unto them about three thousand souls. And they continued steadfastly in the apostles' doctrine and fellowship, and in breaking of bread, and in prayers."* (Acts 2:41, 42)

Bible logic would further lead me to believe that I should err in being overly cautious on the side of getting everyone saved I can, rather than on the side of being afraid the newly

LACK OF SOUL WINNING, BIBLE, AND PRAYER

saved might really not mean it.

Several students with whom I've talked in Christian colleges have let me know they were kids who "got saved" and baptized several times just for the attention, and then, one time it wasn't just for the attention. And, now, lo and behold, the kid no one thought was serious (and perhaps he wasn't at one time) is now studying to be a preacher, Christian school teacher, or missionary.

Most of the time when I'm tempted to think, "Do they really mean it?" about someone's newly-saved convert, it's because I'm not seeing souls won.

Let's go tell 'em and not put "our part" above that of the Holy Spirit. If you truly don't have an opportunity to follow up, don't let the Devil make you so cautious (scared) that you don't even give the person the Gospel to keep him out of Hell.

Do you suppose that by being overly cautious on the "Let's-be-sure-he's-serious" side, we're overemphasizing the human part and underemphasizing the Holy Spirit's part? He can always follow up. *"...Understandest thou what thou readest? And he said, How can I, except some man should guide me? And he desired Philip that he would come up and sit with him. The place of the scripture which he read was this, He was led as a sheep to the slaughter; and like a lamb dumb before his shearer, so opened he not his mouth: In his humiliation his judgment was taken away: and who shall declare his generation? for his life is taken from the earth. And the eunuch answered Philip, and said, I pray thee, of whom speaketh the prophet this? of himself, or of some other man? Then Philip opened his mouth...and preached unto him Jesus. And as they went on their way, they came unto a certain water: and the eunuch said, See, here is water; what doth hinder me to be baptized? And Philip said, If thou believest with all thine heart, thou mayest. And he answered and said, I believe that Jesus Christ is the Son of God. And he commanded the chariot to stand still: and they went down both into the water, both Philip and the eunuch; and he baptized him. And when they were come up out of the water, the Spirit of the Lord caught away Philip, that the eunuch saw him no more: and he went on his way rejoicing. But Philip was found at Azotus: and passing through he preached in all the cities, till he came to Cæsarea.*" (Acts 8:30b–40)

Now around First Baptist Church, many young people who are saved are trained all Sunday long and, in some cases, other days too in order to teach them how to win souls, as well as to play sports, to cook, to sew, to sing, to have Christian fun, and so many other things. But, there are some who get saved who won't stand still long enough for you to teach them. If they believed, the Bible shows they'll go to Heaven whether or not they'll get rewards.

So often the Holy Spirit leads our people to folks who accepted Christ years ago, and it's exciting to see the Holy Spirit doing His part so beautifully as He brings another messenger to them to help them find assurance of salvation and/or to help them grow in grace.

If you're afraid that you will cause people to think they're saved when they're really not, be sure you are not the one that tells them they're saved. Point them to Romans 10:9 after leading them to Jesus and ask them to tell you what they are if they have confessed and believed. "Then you are what?"

"Saved."

"*That if thou shalt confess with thy mouth the Lord Jesus, and shalt believe in thine heart that God hath raised him from the dead, thou shalt be saved.*" (Romans 10:9)

Is your caution on the side of making sure everyone has an opportunity to accept Christ, or is your caution on the side of being afraid you are acting too quickly?

I'm afraid the fact is that not many of us are really that worried about whether or not they're really saved. We just don't want to do our job as a Christian, so we rationalize away the clear Scriptural commands of God's Word.

What do you think?

Wanted: Soul Winners for Such a Time as This

Surely there has never been a better time in the world for soul winning than is this time in which we are living! Now, of course, my head knows, *"...behold, now is the accepted time; behold, now is the day of salvation."* (II Corinthians 6:2) My head knows every time is a good time for soul winning. Every day is the day to tell someone how to go to Heaven.

However, as every year seems to plunge more people into the throes of social isolation, alcoholism, drug addiction, marital problems, sex-related diseases, child-rearing problems, all kinds of abuse, and in the midst of them all, plain old loneliness, more than ever we know Christ is the answer.

Lonely People Need Jesus

People, sitting in the midst of luxury and high-powered jobs, go to their highly touted psychiatrists when their children want to drop out of school, have no goals in school, lose job after job, and they come away from their expensive sessions as bewildered as ever—and oh, so lonely. In rearing their children, they have followed the world's advice about discipline, about religion, education, and sex. They're beginning to suspect the world has no answers. They're much more ready for us to talk to them about Jesus and God's Word. *"...their soul is melted because of trouble. They reel to and fro, and stagger like a drunken man, and are at their wit's end."* (Psalms 107:26b-27)

Children of the middle class go to their places and use their latchkeys to open the door to the apartment or house Mom and Dad are both working to provide. Oftentimes, only one parent is in the home and, of course, is worn to a frazzle when work time is over. The parents know their child needs something to do and are very happy for someone to take him to church and church-related activities.

Not many kids are allowed to go to the work place with the parents as so many used to do on farms and in small businesses. B O R E D is the name of the game with many children and teenagers. They know they need something, but they don't know they need Jesus for time and eternity.

Ghetto kids are seen hanging from high-rise windows, lounging on the curb in front of the building, or aimlessly sitting on the front porch if they're in a row house. Elevators and streets are their unsafe playgrounds. They want something to do so badly that they do "elevator surfing" (riding on the tops of the elevators). Numbers of young people have been killed doing this.

Often older folks have no place to go. Whereas big families stayed in the same area, now siblings don't know each others' addresses and certainly don't get together to plan how to fix Mom's roof or how care for aging family members can be shared by children and grandchildren. When a care center is found, the older people are left with no visitors to feel so lonely that they are ready to talk to anyone who happens to visit.

There are divorced people who now say they would rather be in a poor marriage than to experience the loneliness after the legal proceedings have ended their marriage.

The constant use of television as a tranquilizer has caused children and parents to feel so isolated from each other since they've never discussed real topics. They've never really known each other.

All the wonderful inventions in the world of transportation and technology in the past 50 years have probably been greater for industry and research than they have been for relationships between or among people.

Because fewer people use the Bible at all today, they are thrilled to hear, for the first time, those great truths and even little Bible stories some have not heard since Sunday school days. Yes, today, when men admit they are searching for something, Someone (the Holy Spirit) is working in convicting power. We can let Him work in our hearts to lead us to the field which is ripe unto harvest.

Surely, this is the day that the Lord hath made to tell people, *"For God so loved the world, that He gave His only begotten Son, that whosoever believeth in him should not perish, but have everlasting life."* (John 3:16)

You ask me if Christians are never lonely and are always free from the problems I've mentioned. Certainly, they are sometimes lonely, and Christians have not been promised exemption from suffering, but knowing the beginning from the end, knowing they are Heaven-bound and experiencing the comfort of the Lord as they go through those problems takes the main thrust out of the pain. They know they will never be separated from the most important Person in their lives.

"Who shall separate us from the love of Christ? shall tribulation, or distress, or persecution, or famine, or nakedness, or peril, or sword? As it is written, For thy sake we are killed all the day long; we are accounted as sheep for the slaughter. Nay, in all these things we are more than conquerors through him that loved us. For I am persuaded, that neither death, nor life, nor angels, nor principalities, nor powers, nor things present, nor things to come, Nor height, nor depth, nor any other creature, shall be able to separate us from the love of God, which is in Christ Jesus our Lord." (Romans 8:35–39) It seems that people are lonelier than ever. Want a job? Be a soul winner.

Dying People Need Jesus

Since we're all dying people speaking to dying people, we know everyone needs the Lord. Again, this has always been so! However, it seems to me as if there used to be more people who could tell a dying person how to know he or she was going to Heaven when death of the body took place.

Hospices and counselors are trained to help the dying and their families and friends get to the point of death but usually offer no hope for them after death.

Didn't hospitals used to allow just about anyone who would or could to talk to a dying person? Now, they don't want to disturb the dying by letting a Christian nurse come by to tell them about Heaven. WANTED: Soul winners for such a time as this when even Christian doctors, nurses, and medical support people are not allowed to give spiritual help on hospital time.

People have been told, even by "religious folks," that there is no way to know whether or not they're going to Heaven. It seems to me that soul winners are needed more than ever before. People are ready for them. WANTED: Soul winners to tell the dying, *"For by grace are ye saved through faith; and that not of yourselves: it is the gift of God: Not of works, lest any man should boast."* (Ephesians 2:8, 9)

How sad when "a man or woman of the cloth" is able to get to the dying only to say, "you can't be sure what will be after death." How horrible not to know, *"And this is the record, that God hath given to us eternal life, and this life is in his Son. He that hath the Son hath life; and he that hath not the Son of God hath not life. These things have I written unto you that believe on the name of the Son of God; that ye may know that ye have eternal life, and that ye may believe on the name of the Son of God."* (I John 5:11-13)

WANTED: Soul winners for such a time as this to tell the people that all are sinners and that *"...all have sinned, and come short of the glory of God."* (Romans 3:23)

WANTED: Soul winners to tell them that sin has to be paid for. *"For the wages of sin is death; but the gift of God is eternal life through Jesus Christ our Lord."* (Romans 6:23)

WANTED: Soul winners to let them know God has paid

for their sin and that all they have to do is to take His free gift. *"But God commendeth his love toward us, in that, while we were yet sinners, Christ died for us."* (Romans 5:8) He made it easy to accept His offer, because the Lord is *"...not willing that any should perish."* (II Peter 3:9)

WANTED: Soul winners to tell the people that God's Word says, *"That if thou shalt confess with thy mouth the Lord Jesus, and shalt believe in thine heart that God hath raised him from the dead, thou shalt be saved. For with the heart man believeth unto righteousness; and with the mouth confession is made unto salvation. For whosoever shall call upon the name of the Lord shall be saved."* (Romans 10:9, 10, 13)

If all people are lonely and dying people, soul winners have come for such a time as this.

Soul Winners Are the True V.I.P.'s!

The lady who can tell people how to go to Heaven when they die even has beautiful feet. I've never thought feet were pretty, but God's Word says, *"...How beautiful are the feet of them that preach the gospel of peace, and bring glad tidings of good things!"* (Romans 10:15b)

I love Esther. In Esther 4:14, when her Uncle Mordecai suggested to her *"who knoweth whether thou art come to the kingdom for such a time as this?"* to save her people, she answered, *"...and if I perish, I perish."* (Esther 4:16c)

Soul winners truly are the instruments used of God to give the plan of salvation which will rescue people.

I have found the answer for lack of self-esteem. *"But ye shall receive power, after that the Holy Ghost is come upon you: and ye shall be witnesses unto me both in Jerusalem, and in all Judæa, and in Samaria, and unto the uttermost part of the earth."* (Acts 1:8)

I have found the answer to an empty nest (no child or children) or empty-nest syndrome (children having left home).

The people who consider themselves victims of these problems can help as many people as they can to be born again. *"...Except a man be born again, he cannot see the kingdom of God."* (John 3:3b)

I have found the answer to the singles' problem. It isn't anything new. In fact, it's a commission given hundreds of years ago. *"Go ye therefore, and teach all nations, baptizing them in the name of the Father, and of the Son, and of the Holy Ghost: Teaching them to observe all things whatsoever I have commanded you: and, lo, I am with you alway, even unto the end of the world."* (Matthew 28:19, 20)

Single ladies who are involved in teaching folks how to go to Heaven when they die and then, involved in teaching those who have accepted Jesus to observe all things Jesus commanded are fulfilled, excited, interesting, creative people. And, they are never alone—*"...lo, I am with you alway, even unto the end of the world. Amen."* (Matthew 28:20b)

A Soul Winner Has Such a Balanced Life

God certainly gave a plan that brings fulfillment, a sense of importance, excitement, mental stimulation, spiritual growth, social interaction, and even sometimes physical exercise.

So often, the soul winner's convert wants to have the whole Bible explained as he or she is taken to be taught soul winning. The two (the soul winner and the convert) usually do pray and talk about the things of the Lord between visits they might be making or, to and from the site of the soul winning time together. Truly, a new convert is a real source of motivation for getting into or staying in the Word of God.

All of this leads to a balanced life.

Wanted: Soul Winners

Soul winners are about to become an endangered species as leaders are making excuses for Christians to retreat from the

Lack of Soul Winning, Bible, and Prayer

field as fast as they can. Therefore, soul winners are needed more than ever before.

I recall the story I have heard about Dr. John R. Rice, who after winning a soul at Pacific Garden Mission in Chicago, said he didn't want to continue studying at the University of Chicago in order to be a college history teacher. He felt there was nothing to compare to winning souls and offered himself to God full-time for just that. How many times I've seen that good man and his wife walk up to someone to sweetly ask them if they would like to know how to be saved.

If you get a thrill out of reaping a harvest on a farm or in a vegetable garden, if you enjoy pulling up nets full of fish from the river, if you like to watch ripples made by the throwing of a rock into a lake, if you get excited about papers returned to you from another state after releasing tract-filled balloons or after throwing tract-filled bottles into an ocean, you cannot imagine the excitement and fulfillment of winning a soul to Christ. Get ready to live the abundant life. *"I am come that they might have life, and that they might have it more abundantly."* (John 10:10)

You never know from whence the blessings are coming. One day recently one of the *Christian Womanhood* office workers called to say that a lady had phoned for help because her husband had said he was going to leave her. When two other ladies and I went to the address given, God allowed us to see her accept Christ. She later told us that she had just gone down the telephone directory looking for the word "Christian" and had found Christian Womanhood. When her husband came home at the end of his shift, we found that he didn't mind our being there at all. You see, some of our college girls had won him to Jesus by a laundromat seventeen years before when he was eight years old. What a thrill to take up from there.

On January 1, 1990, my father-in-law went to be with

Jesus. I was sitting in the Intensive Care Unit waiting room when a little lady began to strike up a conversation with me. I thought, "Oh Lord, I should tell her how to get saved, and I'm so tired. I was going to lie down here." Before I could finish the thought, she began to tell me about her husband's dying, her son just having been killed in an accident, and about some people (who I later discovered were our graduates) having led them to Jesus several years ago. The soul winners no longer live in this area, but I called to tell them about my experience. What a way to live!

I Have a New Program!

Yes, I have a new program for singles. It's new only because so few use it. It's Matthew 28:19, 20. I have a new program for the widows, the full-time Christian workers' wives, the separated and divorced ladies, and the childless. It's only new because it's so rarely practiced. It's Matthew 28:19-20. If what you're doing isn't for time and eternity, forget it! Join the new program. If you have to "make tents," don't allow "tent making" to be your life. "...*for by their occupation they were tentmakers.*" (Acts 18:3b) Tent making should be a tool to be able to do "time and eternity" work. This "new" program causes us to look at people so differently. If a child accidentally breaks a lamp, just think, "Does that lamp have an eternal soul?" If a teenager puts a dent into the bumper of your new car, perhaps you'll at least ask if he was hurt before you lash out at him. Does that car have a soul?

WANTED: Soul winners for such a time as this!

God Gave...So Can You!"

Do you ever wonder like I do, "What could I ever do for Jesus to show Him how much I love Him for giving Himself for me?" I believe I know the answer although I do not know enough about it to practice it consistently. The answer is

"GIVE YOURSELF AWAY!" You ask, "How?" God gives us examples through His birth, life, death, burial, and resurrection as it is found in the Word of God.

Give Yourself to the Word of God!

Most of us are so ignorant of the Word of God that it is no wonder that we think the term "give yourself" is strange. Supposedly mature Christians sometimes even think living a life without retaliation or with strong separation is weird. Because our thinking is determined by what we allow to enter into our minds, the worldly seems right, and the spiritual seems wrong. *"There is a way which seemeth right unto a man, but the end thereof are the ways of death."* (Proverbs 14:12)

When I'd want to go to a school dance or something similar, my mom used to tell me, "Grandma Wilkins always said the church is dancing into the world, and the world is dancing into the church until you can't see the difference." As I sulked away thinking, "Grandma Wilkins Schmilkins...who cares what some old lady said? She's dead anyway! She didn't know anything!" Little did I know I'd someday be begging Christian kids to set their affection on things above and be hid with Christ in God. (Please read Colossians 3:1–4.)

A million times a day I say, "That doesn't sound right." However, I've begun to realize I don't know what is right and what is wrong, because I'm so ignorant of the only Book that can teach me eternal rights and wrongs. Oh, yes, I've studied the Book, read through it, and have loved it. However, considering the number of years I have been saved, I'm relatively unlearned. Are *you?* Hey, then, I know something we can give Jesus...we can give ourselves *to* His Word.

The fact that I did not give myself *to* the Word earlier in life has been *my* biggest regret. One time I was evaluating the number of Scripture verses I would know if *my* Bible were ever taken from me, and found that I was pitifully lacking.

For some time I have been trying to live in the Word. My way of "living in the Word" seems so simple that I've always been embarrassed to tell it; however, I'm beginning to think my little way is better than your way if *you* have no way at all. Maybe *my* way would be a start for those of *you* who are still complaining, "I don't have time to live in the Word," or "I just don't understand the Bible," or "I read the Bible for a while, but then I don't get anything from it and quit."

I've been through that off-again, on-again syndrome that goes something like this: *No* Bible; a revival meeting; read Bible avidly for three days; read Bible one day not being able to concentrate or get anything from it, give up; no Bible; revival; then again I read Bible for three days, ad nauseam.

Today, people do not have enough character to do something if they aren't receiving from what they're doing. They quit! The worldly philosophy even tells us to be true to ourselves by giving up that which doesn't mean anything to us. I want to tell you I've known some good habits that have helped me even when I wasn't sincere.

True, we should find a way to read the Bible until it does mean something, but we're commanded to stay in it whether it does or not. *"Study to shew thyself approved unto God, a workman that needeth not to be ashamed, rightly dividing the word of truth."* (II Timothy 2:15) However, since we are all horribly affected by the world, it is even more important than ever to see to it that we allow the Holy Spirit to teach and reach us through His Word. We need to be thrilled and excited as we get our joys, laughs, tears, shocks, facts, truths, and all other needs from the Scripture. (II Timothy 3:16, 17)

You still want *to* know *my* way? I don't know if I want *to* tell *you*. I read just a few verses (maybe only three or four) instead of many chapters. I really ask myself questions about those few verses, "What does this mean? How does it apply *to* me? Does this mean like the time I did such and such?" Then, I sit and

Lack of Soul Winning, Bible, and Prayer

let *my* mind wander on purpose, just visiting with the Lord.

One day when I was on John 14:1–7, I specialized on mansions, thinking about mansions I have seen here on earth and thanking Him for the one I can't even imagine in Heaven. I thanked the Lord for a trip *to* the Arbor Lodge Mansion in Nebraska City, Nebraska, and prayed for the people who took me on that trip...*my* parents! Then, I thought of someone who doesn't have a heavenly mansion, because she's not saved. I prayed for her. I know we need a prayer list *to* check *to* see that we're praying for all those for whom we promised we'd pray. We also need *to* have Bible study. However, this grabbing a few verses or even a portion of one small verse *to* chew on all day long will thrill your heart, cause *you to* glory in the Word and provoke *you to* further study.

One day I was dwelling on Philippians 3:10 (and more especially in the phrase *"that I may know Him"*) and therefore spent every few hours thinking about and praising God for a different way through which I knew Him. I could see Him really well every way I turned.

I remember spending a week in Romans 8:35–39, which features sheep. I thought *to* pray for people who came *to my* mind for the first time in years as I recalled the one time I even saw a sheep shearing on a farm in Thayer, Kansas. I also prayed a lot for India, Africa, and the people of Asia as I spent some time considering the word "famine."

I just let Him talk *to* me through His Word, and I talk *to* Him about that which His Word reminds me. It's just like talking *to* a friend. My Friend says something that reminds me to tell Him something. I even interrupt Him! You see, we're quite close.

Many of us run through six chapters and a prayer list in such a perfunctory manner that there is no way we can possibly get anything from it. This method is somewhat like our running up to a friend to say, "I got your letter; I'll skip through it, bye now." They would think we were crazy, and that kind of relationship wouldn't last long. Neither will your relationship with God last if it is carried on through these puny methods.

Stop, think out each word, speak the phrases aloud, draw out a word such as, "all" in *"I can do all things…"*; then ask yourself, "How can I do all things?" Answer yourself, "Through Christ."

"Through Christ Who does what?"

"Who strengtheneth me!" Dear me, I'm letting you know how much I talk to myself again! Well, I've decided there's no help for it, but I hope my musings help you decide to give a gift to Jesus and get into His Word!

PART THREE

*The Antidote
for the Five Sins of Christian Women*

There are antidotes for the poison of the five sins! Study and learn them.

- **Read and pray!** *"Study to shew thyself approved unto God, a workman that needeth not to be ashamed, rightly dividing the word of truth."* (II Timothy 2:15)

  "Pray without ceasing." (I Thessalonians 5:17)

- **Accept life as it always will be.** Especially do we need to accept the "three S's" which Mrs. Beverly Hyles calls "life's inescapables"—self, sacrifice, and suffering. Accept correction as love. *"For whom the LORD loveth he correcteth."* (Proverbs 3:12)

- **Bury what you cannot change.** Many of us still excuse ourselves from any responsibility of committing the five sins on the grounds of our past, physical attributes, temperament, or 1,001 other things over which we feel we have no control. If we really truly don't have control to change one or more of these things in our lives, let's have a funeral in order to bury them. *"Forgetting those things which are behind, and reaching forth unto those things which are before."* (Philippians 3:13b)

- **Run from the scene of temptation until you can return to handle it rationally.** If you cannot leave bodily, at least leave the situation mentally. *"There hath no temptation taken you but such as is common to man: but God is faithful, who will not suffer you to be tempted above that ye are able; but will with the temptation also make a way to escape, that ye may be able to bear it."* (I Corinthians 10:13)

- **Stay!** Stay by people, jobs, churches, and schools—imperfect as they are. If you are leaving something or someone because of the frailties of humans, you really have no place else to go. You'll just run into another set of human frailties. I have often wanted to run, but I could never get a satisfactory answer to the question, "Where?" If you get upset with teachers at your children's Christian school and change to another Christian school, I am afraid you will just find another set of problems. Besides that, your children will be learning well the lesson, "If you don't get along, leave." What if he or she follows that example with a spouse? We'd better stay in the tunnel and look toward the end where there is light instead of trying to live in the light only to end up in a tunnel. In other words, we need to stay by people when they don't understand us; we need to work through our problems in that Sunday school class or bus route!

- **Laugh!** Laugh at funny things, at unfunny things, and especially at yourself. Laughing at yourself will cause you great joy for you will never run out of material!

Line Upon Line and Precept Upon Precept!

Let me share some more little helps; one of them might help you, and another might help someone else. In fact, some of them may seem to be the very same principle.

I.
Saturate Yourself with Scripture!

Saturate yourself with Scripture—not just any Scripture but a particular dose for the particular problem. Memorizing Scripture is saturating or permeating yourself with verses. *"Wherewithal shall a young man cleanse his way? by taking heed thereto according to thy word...Thy word have I hid in mine heart that I might not sin against thee."* (Psalms 119:9, 11) Then when you start to lose control and feel the beginning of a temper tantrum or you get critical or you start to feel depressed, force yourself to quote these verses that will help give you victory.

If you go to bed at night, and negative thoughts come to your mind, you won't have to get up and get the Bible; just quote the verses you have memorized. The verses that counteract that negative thinking will be right on the surface of your mind, and you can start saying them in your mind.

Saturate yourself with doses of Scripture that fit and will help remedy your problem. Either type or write those verses on cards and post them wherever you are—above your sink, above the bathtub, on your ironing board, on the mirror, so you can memorize as you work. Some of you will say, "I don't have time."

Yes, you do! You can have verses in the car—over the visor or steering wheel. When you are sitting and waiting for traffic or trains, you won't become frustrated and impatiently say, "When is this traffic going to move? I've got to be at that meeting!" Saying that will not accomplish anything. Instead, you can say, "Thank You, Lord! This will give me more time for memorizing the Scripture. Thank You, Lord! Thank You! Thank You!"

When you have to go to the doctor's office, have these verses with you. If you have to wait an hour, it won't seem that long because you have had a goal that you have been able to reach. Saturate yourself with a dose of Scripture that is appropriate to the problem you are trying to overcome. If it is not a train that causes a delay, it is something else! Don't plan on your plan working right! Charlie "Tremendous" Jones, the author of *Life Is Tremendous,* says, "Plan on your plan not working, and someday if your plan does work, then you can work that into your schedule, too."

Anything that comes between you and your goal causes frustration. Don't plan on that goal of getting to the doctor's office without an obstacle—like a train. Be prepared, and you won't be frustrated! Say, "God, through these things that seem to be opposing me, help me work this opposition so that it will be used rightly; and it will be a blessing." If you don't work on this attitude, by the time you get across the railroad tracks, others will wish you hadn't crossed the tracks! People, let's realize these frustrations will happen.

"Saturate yourself" means to read the verses over and over

until they are a part of you. They will leap to your mind the instant you need them!

II.
Use Substitute Thinking with Bible-Taught Thoughts!

Substitute thinking has been a helpful principle for me. When a negative thought comes in on me, I grab a "Philippians 4:8" thought and bring it to mind. As I mentioned before, I have found that a person can think only one thought at a time. I have also learned substitute thinking must be consciously practiced day after day.

The way a person can have victorious Christian living is to have victorious Christian thinking! Substitute thinking is substituting a positive thought for a negative thought. In other words, immediately replace a negative thought with a positive, Bible-taught thought. When a negative thought comes like, "I don't think I can do all I'm going to have to do tomorrow," that is when you need a positive thought to replace this defeating negative thought. When you can't sleep at night, you will be able to program yourself to sleep at night. Perhaps you are tense, and you wonder why you can't sleep. You don't even trust your head to the pillow! The reason you can't sleep is that negative thoughts are filling your mind!

The negative thinking continues, "I don't think I can do all that I must do tomorrow. It is already late, and I'm not going to get enough sleep. I'm going to be so tired in the morning." And sure enough, you are! Don't be surprised! That is exactly what is going to happen.

Reprogram your mind! Think of something that you are going to do for others. When you go to bed at night, program yourself: "I am going to get up in the morning, and this is what I am planning to do for someone." Following this principle will relax you. Possibly you won't get much sleep if you go to bed with a relaxed state of mine, but you will get excited about what you are going to do for God. Ask God to help you do that

THE ANTIDOTE

with substitute thinking. When that negative thought comes, then quickly grab a positive thought.
* Remember the soul you won to Christ.
* Remember how good you felt when you baked a cake for someone who was sick.
* Compose a note to write as soon as you get up. Plan the couple of sentences to someone telling him how much you appreciate him.

I can promise that your head will automatically relax against the pillow. You will trust your head to the pillow. Remember, next time you cannot seem to relax yourself or allow yourself to relax, use substitute thinking!

III.
Put Your Magnifying Glass on the Right Side!

Put the magnifying glass principle into effect. Magnify that thought which is on the right side—the positive side. Neglect the seeming need to place the magnifying glass on the left or negative side. I have noticed that some women put the magnifying glass on the left side; they only see the bad points of everyone and every situation. They major constantly on the negative. No matter where you see them, they have a perpetual frown creasing their foreheads. They see absolutely the worst in every situation. Yes, there is a time to have critical constructive evaluation concerning a situation. However, the person who puts the magnifying glass on the left-hand side usually sees only what is wrong and bad.

There are those people who are happy all the time. They seem to put their magnifying glass on the right side constantly—to every situation and to every person. They see nothing but good in their husbands, or they say nothing but good about their husbands, and they see nothing but good in other people. If you start saying anything negative, they come back with something good and positive! I guess I am asking you to be like a Pollyanna Whittier and open your mind and heart to everything that should be helped and that needs to be better. Like Pollyanna who played the "glad game," I am asking that you *"Rejoice in the Lord alway: and again I say, Rejoice!"*

Now there are times when we should see the bad, such as when we are in a counseling situation and have the opportunity to help another. We should not overlook sin, but the only person we can talk to about sin is that one we are counseling. A counselor has no right to share with someone else.

I challenge you to put your magnifying glass on the right side. Decide you are going to magnify all those things that are going to help you do a better and greater job for God. You will paralyze yourself by putting your magnifying glass on the left side—even to scrutinize yourself. If you see your own weaknesses all the time and none of your strengths, you will paralyze yourself. You cannot be an effective Christian if you cripple yourself.

The "magnifying glass principle" and "substitute thinking" are about the same. Some will want to use one idea, and some will want to apply the other. Both of these are to help you control what you want or allow to stay in your mind. Sometimes you cannot help what comes into your mind, but you can help what you allow to stay in your mind. Certainly, you can be careful what you allow yourself to see and hear; that is what separation from the world is all about.

IV.
Take a Mini-Vacation!

Mentally remove yourself from the negative situation or thought. Do you remember a time in your life in which you felt an unbelievable peace and contentment? Go back there—not to stay or to escape reality; just stay a few minutes in order to come back to the task at hand feeling refreshed and renewed.

When I first began speaking about "The Five Sins of

The Antidote

Christian Women," God allowed me to go to Hawaii. I enjoyed the time over there so much. Can you believe that we had the most beautiful New Year's service on the beach? I can remember how the ocean seemed at night and how warm it was with the ocean breezes. Sometimes when I become tired, or when there's a disappointment, or I'm not making my goal, I take a "10-minute break" to Hawaii and relive a bit of that time on that Hawaiian beach.

If you are the type of person who wants to withdraw from reality all of the time, I wouldn't advise this method for you. If you can learn to take a few minutes for a "mini-vacation" and come back and talk with your children, your college roommate, or your husband rationally, it will be a blessing to your lives. Removing yourself from the situation is another way of gaining control of yourself.

I don't know where your place might be, but for awhile my place was the mountains of North Carolina where my husband was a pastor. One afternoon when I needed a mini-vacation, I went to the mountains and sat there for about two hours. I could feel the calmness creep into me as I looked at those mountains and realized that they would be there forever and ever. My problems seemed so small as I looked at those mountains. For some, that special place may be the ocean or a lake.

Do you remember a time when you were relaxed and at peace with God, with the world, and with yourself? It seemed as if you were victorious at that time. Let's say that you are now in the midst of a big chaotic time, and you feel yourself going. That is exactly the time to "remove yourself" for a few minutes. Don't remove yourself from reality. Face reality, but remove yourself for a few minutes in order to come back to the problem rested and relaxed. You can enjoy that few minutes as you relive a mini-vacation. I believe when you go on a true vacation with the Lord, the real result of the vacation comes years later as you are able to remember and to enjoy those

The Five Sins of Christian Women

times when you were on that vacation.

Practice these principles. God has given us a mind we can use. We can even play games with ourselves in order to get some rest and relaxation whenever we need it whether or not we are working.

V.
Put Others First!

Put others first. Challenge yourself to think of ten things you could do to keep others from becoming negative and do them. Our preacher, Dr. Jack Hyles, taught, "Happiness is helping others and living for others." Then he stretched out his hands. Happiness is giving to others. Then Brother Hyles pulled in his hands to show morbid introspection. "How do *I* think about things? How do *I* feel?"

Every Christian should perform a certain type of self-examination, but far too many of us just tear ourselves apart. We have the mistaken concept that perhaps this self-analysis and soul searching will help us to be a better person; instead it ruins us and hurts us more. Such self-examination can keep us from looking outside ourselves. It is not enough not to be arrogant. It is not enough just to refuse to be proud.

Some people say, "It is not that I'm thinking about myself. I don't think that I'm good." Thinking of yourself as being bad is just as wrong. Don't think about yourself at all. Think of others. What can you do for someone else? How can you encourage someone else?

Think for a moment: how many times do you write notes? Our girls at Hyles-Anderson College write notes such as, "I saw you today, and I wanted you to know that I thought you looked especially pretty." Words like these help so much! How many of you send notes to one another? You could tell someone, "I didn't just think this when I was with you, but I thought of it when I was away from you, too." Keep a notepad handy and start writing notes to the Preacher and tell him what you liked in his sermon. Be an encouragement. Be someone on whom he can count! Always be building him instead of tearing him down for not fulfilling all of your expectations.

Being specific in writing notes can encourage and influence another in ways we never dream.

- Tell the person what certain thing she did or said that affected you.
- Tell the person how she affected you, such as, "When you told about…"
- Give a quote that the person has said back to her. Often, she doesn't even know she said what you are quoting.
- Tell the person what you did for someone because of what you saw her do for another.
- Tell the person about a good conversation you had based on what you heard her say.
- Tell the person how you used a recipe or an idea she gave you and what the ramifications were.
- Tell the person what you have heard someone else say good about her.
- Remind the person of something good she did or said many weeks, months, or years ago.
- Tell the person of a Scripture verse of which she reminds you.
- Send the person a good cartoon, a joke, or poem that reminds you of a good time with her.

VI.
"In Everything Give Thanks!"

Give thanks. In a difficult situation, start looking for things about which you can say, "Thank You, Lord," for everything that happens to you. "Thank You. I don't know why this happened, but I know everything that happens to me is for my good and Your glory." Compose lists of ten things, ten people,

The Five Sins of Christian Women

ten great days, etc. for which you thank the Lord.

"*In every thing give thanks: for this is the will of God in Christ Jesus concerning you.*" (I Thessalonians 5:18) "Thank You, Lord, that You allowed me to have this trouble, that You trusted me with it, and that You think that I am going to be able to cope with it. Lord, I know that with You, I can cope with this very thing."

VII.
"Pray Without Ceasing!"

"Pray about everything; worry about nothing."

"*I beseech you therefore, brethren, by the mercies of God, that ye present your bodies a living sacrifice, holy, acceptable unto God, which is your reasonable service. And be not conformed to this world: but be ye transformed by the renewing of your mind, that ye may prove what is that good, and acceptable, and perfect, will of God.*" (Romans 12:1, 2) I believe our problem as Christian women is not giving our bodies as living sacrifices. Have you ever had that time in your life when you gave yourself to the Lord? I know some of you have given your souls to the Lord, you have accepted Christ as your Saviour, and you are on your way to Heaven. But have you had that time in your life when you said, "I give myself to the Lord Jesus; I want Him to be the Master of my life"?

Now sometimes after you have had that time, you will take yourself back. You say, "Monday I gave myself to the Lord. I had that time of dedication; but, by 11:00 the next morning I had taken myself back again."

As quickly as you recognize that fact, don't wait a minute! Just say, "Lord, I don't want myself back. I took myself back, but I don't want myself back. Cleanse me." Please do this. He wants you to give yourself again. Say, "I'm sorry, Lord, that I allowed this situation to come through my mind." Perhaps you don't even know what made you take yourself back. Maybe someone said something negative to you, and you didn't realize what an effect it had on you! It will affect you every time! You took yourself back and allowed yourself to entertain a thought of bitterness, so once again give your mind back to Him. Say, "Here I am again, Lord; take me." Practice, practice, practice! Each time it will last a little bit longer. Practice in order to have a victorious Christian life through victorious Christian thinking.

Being nervous, worried, depressed; gossiping, griping, and being critical; not loving your family; not going soul winning or reading your Bible will not happen if we are doing these positive things. Say to yourself over and over, "I am going to be different from the ordinary Christian woman."

Girls, you don't want to be as the ordinary Christian woman that you've seen, do you? Then you are going to have to practice being different. You are going to have to give yourselves back to God over and over again. Every time you take yourself back, for example, when your eyes watch something wrong, when your mouth says something wrong, you are going to have to give yourself back to the Lord. Ask God to help you to be different. If you practice being a different girl, you won't be depressed or gossip, gripe, and complain. You may not become a great woman who will go down in the history books, but you can be a "woman used of God." This should be your constant prayer. Is that your main cry? To be used of God is my desire! If this is your cry, you will be able to *"Rejoice in the Lord alway: and again I say, Rejoice."* Rejoice in the **Lord**—not in your troubles.

We fight so much about ourselves. We cry so much over ourselves. Cry over others! Cry because you are touched by the Lord, but don't cry over yourself.

It Is a Weakness to Cry Over Yourself, But It Is a Strength to Cry Over Others.

Most women are just sitting around saying, "I don't know what I'm going to do! I've just had all these problems; in fact, I don't know how I'm going to make it through the day!" You make it through this day because according to Philippians 4:13, you "can do all things through Christ which strengtheneth you." That's how!

He supplies everything you need. That's how you make it through this day and every other day. Every time you throw up your hands in despair, cry over hurt feelings, and cry about yourself, you are weakening your testimony before your family and before everyone else. Oh, we need a group of different women, just people who will be different. Some of you know that I have a burden about being different, not odd, (although we will seem odd, won't we?) but being different-from-the ordinary Christian woman. Someone else needs to take that burden!

One day about two and one-half years ago when I was in a meeting, a woman stood up and said, "We don't have many great women." I thought, "That's true." I started thinking and questioning, "Should there be great women as we have great men of God?" I came to the conclusion that yes, I believe we ought to have men of God for girls to look to, but there also should be ladies after whom they can pattern their lives.

Girls believe the women's lib lingo because they want to be something themselves. They feel that in order to do something, they have to act as a man acts—instead of being a Proverbs 31 lady. Let's show them they can be real ladies, serving, doing everything that God would want them to do, with the older teaching the younger, counseling, and bearing burdens with one another. Help them see the many ways in which they could be great—not what this world terms as "great," but to "be a woman used of God."

The Antidote

That term, "to be used of God," has gone through my mind and through my being as I've thought and prayed, "To be used of God, to sing, to speak, to pray," or "to wash dishes, to change diapers, to be used of God." Bible women were used of God. Jochebed yielded her son; Deborah rallied the Israelites; Ruth heeded the advice of her mother-in-law; Esther risked her life for her people; Mary, the mother of Jesus, was obedient; Anna watched faithfully for her Messiah; Dorcas used a needle; Rhoda believed; and Lois and Eunice patiently passed on their faith. These were just a few of the women mentioned in the Bible who used what God gave them.

Susanna Wesley was used of God to take care of 19 children, nine of whom died at birth or in infancy. It was said that Susanna was such a dominant force that her influence was indelibly imprinted on her children's personalities.

Katherine von Bora, former nun, married Martin Luther, who was pursued by the Pope, hated by his fellow man, and harassed by religious fanatics. While her husband helped usher in the Reformation, she patiently reared their six children and was a keeper at home.

The daughter of a drunkard, Mary Slessor of Scotland heard about Calabar, Africa. For 38 years, Mary labored in Calabar, Nigeria, traveling where other missionaries feared to go, told cannibals about Jesus, settled disputes between pagan chiefs, walked the same paths as dangerous animals, rescued orphans from certain death, and nursed the sick and dying. She was known as "everybody's Mother" to the natives she loved.

Twenty-five-year-old Ann, the help meet and dedicated wife of missionary and Bible translator Adoniram Judson, left her homeland to minister with her husband in Burma. After the deaths of two children, she gave birth to Roger Williams Judson, who died at the age of eight months. She watched her husband dragged off to jail, won the right to visit him, and smuggled in his Burmese Bible translations. With her health broken, she died at the age of 37.

Elizabeth Alden Scott, the daughter of missionaries serving in China, came to America to pursue an education. In the fall of 1931, she returned to China as a missionary and married John Stam, In September 1934, God gave the Stams a lovely baby daughter. On December 8, 1934, the Communists marched the Stams from their farmhouse, leaving behind their daughter, and took their lives. Shortly before their martyrdom, they cabled the mission headquarters, "May He help us to be satisfied with His plan for this day. May God be glorified whether by life or by death."

Mrs. John R. Rice, Miss Fairy Shappard, Dr. Viola Walden, Mrs. Lee Roberson, and Mrs. Jack Hyles were used greatly in my life. These women were used, not abused—used! If only we were willing to be used in any way that God would want to use us, whether or not it is in the limelight—not caring at all as long as we're being used! This is the kind of woman we ought to be! This is the goal that we all ought to have. **God wants to use us.** It is ridiculous to think that He wouldn't use us—**if** we are usable. So what we Christian ladies want to be is **usable!**

Now some of us get upset if things don't go right, and our plans are changed. The Preacher may ask you to do something and then unexpectedly change his mind. When he tries to explain the new plan, you retort, "Now, look, you told me this, and I'll look bad before the people if you change it." If you start arguing with the man of God, you won't be used! He can't afford to use you—no matter how many talents you have.

When your preacher or your husband says something, you say, "Yes, sir!" Plan later how you are going to work it out. It doesn't matter how you look before the people; it matters how **he** looks before the people. God will vindicate you, too! As you put yourself last, God will put you first! As you put yourself down, God will put you up! As you give up the things that you thought you liked and wanted, He will give you those things that you love and things you had no idea that you would love.

I have found that women don't have any idea of what they want anyway. Half the time they want one thing, and half the time they want something else; desires are so fickle. Only God's Word is stable. A person can be helped so very much not to have a critical spirit if he will just remember one simple verse (and you know by now what it is), *"Rejoice in the Lord alway: and again I say, Rejoice."*

Let's go over some principles once more. You might ask, "Why is she repeating these principles so often?" Somehow, we just don't get them the first time we hear or read something. We need line upon line and precept upon precept. Often I have talked with women when they come to me individually, and they ask, "What do I do about this or that, Marlene?"

I say, "Don't you remember when I taught about this?"

They say, "Oh, yes!" Somehow they hadn't applied it to themselves.

How many ways are there to say **saturate yourself with Scripture?!** There is only one way, ladies. I tell you that the Word of God will cleanse you from sin. It will take care of every problem you have in the whole world, but you have to know it and use it. You have to saturate yourself with Scripture! Keep that very important principle in mind. You must be Scripture saturated!

Then when the hard times come, you will be ready. I have talked with women who have had a baby die of crib death. They checked in on the baby one minute, the baby was all right, and the next minute the baby was dead. What does that grief-stricken mother do? Really, there is only one thing for that mother to do. She must flee to the Word of God and remember those things which are so much in her heart that she cannot separate them from herself. *"Wherewithal shall a young man cleanse his way? by taking heed thereto according to thy word."* (Psalms 119:9) The same is true for the young woman, the middle-aged woman, or the older woman. It doesn't matter what your age; there is only one way you can get help, and that is from the Word of God.

Remember to apply the principle of **substitute thinking!** When a bad negative thought comes to mind, grab a Bible-taught, Philippians 4:8 thought and replace the negative thought in your mind. You can only think one thing at a time.

Remember how to relax yourself by **removing yourself from the situation.** Before you go to bed not trusting your head to the pillow, and getting up as fatigued as when you went to bed, have you relaxed yourself, one finger at a time, and then one toe at a time? I know it sounds funny, but by the time you have told each member of your body to relax, and you get to your head and tell it to relax on the pillow, you'll be asleep. Decide on the purpose that you need rest so that you can do a better job for the Lord, and ask Him to give you that rest. Use a few little things like this to help you.

The **magnifying glass** principle is seeing the good and positive side of every situation and every person.

Put others first! This will help you in every problem you will ever have. We have been talking about loving our husbands. If you put your husband first, you are going to love him.

Are we going to try to save this nation! That sounds like a presumptuous goal. Save the nation?! Save a country?! WOW! Do you know that anyone who has ever had any mark on history has seemingly been a little crazy and a little bit fanatical? They thought they could really do something to save the country! Maybe we ladies won't save this nation, but let's give it all we've got. Let's try! Let's do everything we can, and maybe we will make some mark!

PART FOUR

*The Sixth
Sin of Christian Women*

CHAPTER ONE

Jealousy

> "Jealousy is a tiger that tears not only its prey but also its own raging heart."
> – a proverb

I ONCE ASKED PEOPLE around me, "Am I characterized by jealousy?" I began to think about the times when I was jealous, and I honestly could not think of any. At the time I gave this talk on the sixth sin of Christian women, which is jealousy, our preacher, Dr. Jack Hyles, had given us the assignment to read through the Bible in a year. Because of chemotherapy, when I started reading, I was barely able to focus my eyes or pay attention. It was especially difficult for me to get through the chapters about the kidneys and the gallstones. I was so glad for Joseph and people like him!

When I reached the books of Samuel, Chronicles, and Kings, I became riveted by one story about Solomon where it talks about jealousy. I Kings 3:16-27 says, *Then came there two women, that were harlots, unto the king, and stood before him. And the one woman said, O my lord, I and this woman dwell in one house; and I was delivered of a child with her in the house. And it came to pass the third day after that I was delivered, that this woman was delivered also: and we were together; there was no stranger with us in the house, save we two in the house. And this woman's child died in the night; because she overlaid it. And she arose at midnight, and took my son from beside me, while thine handmaid slept, and laid it in her bosom, and laid her dead child in my bosom. And when I rose in the morning to give my child suck, behold, it was dead: but when I had considered it in the morning, behold, it was not my son, which I did bear. And the other woman said, Nay; but the living is my son, and the dead is thy son. And this said, No; but the dead is thy son, and the living is my son. Thus they spake before the king. Then said the king, The one saith, This is my son that liveth, and thy son is the dead: and the other saith, Nay; but thy son is the dead, and my son is the living. And the king said, Bring me a sword. And they brought a sword before the king. And the king said, Divide the living child in two, and give half to the one, and half to the other. Then spake the woman whose the living child was unto the king, for her bowels yearned upon her son, and she said, O my lord, give her the living child, and in no wise slay it. But the other said, Let ut be neither mine nor thine, but divide it. Then the king answered and said, Give her the living child, and in no wise slay it: she is the mother thereof."*

I had always thought this account was a good story to teach how to be a judge, but I had never thought of dividing anyone. And, I never applied this passage to myself. Have you ever been the cause of dividing anyone? Let's reread verse 22 which says, *"And the other woman said, Nay; but the living is my son, and the dead is thy son. And this said, No; but the dead is thy son, and the living is my son. Thus they spake before the king."*

Don't we women sound exactly like these two women? As Cindy Schaap says, those women are our Biblical counterparts! There are so many possibilities to divide children, especially if there has been a divorce or a separation. Children can also be divided emotionally. Instead of a couple putting down their own hurts and seeing to it that they work out things together, they choose to divide the children. They sacrifice their children in order to salve their own feelings.

How many people have we divided? Jealousy divides. If I have not been jealous in situations, it has been because I saw the warning flag that said, "Jealousy is ahead." I do not know how I saw the warning flag, but I saw the green-eyed monster, and I realized the possibility that I was going to be jealous. Being jealous scares me. The Bible says in Proverbs 6:34, *"For jealousy is the rage of a man: therefore he will not spare in the day of vengeance."* It frightens me to think that a jealous person is a merciless person characterized by a burning, intense, violent anger.

Knowing that makes me wonder if we just don't know or do not realize that we are jealous people. Could it be that we just aren't paying any attention to the warning flag? We are not seeing jealousy down the road, and we are not seeing any way to keep ourselves from being jealous.

Do you think perhaps we don't fight our jealousy because we don't name it for what it is? After all, if you don't name it, then you can't fight it. *"…for love is strong as death;* **jealousy is cruel as the grave:** *the coals thereof are coals of fire, which hath a most vehement flame."* (Song of Solomon 8:6) The following are some of the warning signs I have seen that mark the beginning stages of jealousy:

Reasons Why I Feel Jealous

"I feel inferior."
"I feel insecure."
"I feel dumb."
"I feel awkward."
"I feel put down."
"I feel intimidated."
"I feel sick."
"I feel tired."
"I feel threatened."
"I feel bored."
"I feel ineffective."
"I feel scared."
"I feel lonely."
"I feel weak."
"I feel frustrated."

"I feel disappointed."
"I feel hurt."
"I feel guilty."
"I feel hungry."
"I feel unsure about my appearance."
"I feel like I have too much to do."
"I feel weakened by family members' problems."
"I feel I am being blamed for something."
"I have sinned or I have been sinned against."

If you see and recognize the warning signs, then you will not tear down great people who could become even greater and very good at any important opportunity that comes their way. You can tear people apart just by not watching the warning flag. Sad to say, that is exactly what we do today. If we were to take care of the jealousy and fight it, much of the gossiping and having a critical spirit would disappear.

People, let's just realize that we are human beings and that we are going to have chances for jealousy. Throughout my life, there have been times for jealousy, but I have learned that I have a responsibility not to become jealous. Also, I have a responsibility to relieve others of jealousy.

Once that term "jealousy" is applied to the problem, then the problem can be solved. See, we don't want to take responsibility for anything. Why should anyone be jealous of a beautiful person? Can that person help the fact that God made her beautiful and talented? Should she dress like a bag lady to diminish her beauty? Have you ever noticed that no one is ever jealous over the person who doesn't make good grades, or the person who hasn't been taught how to dress properly, or the terribly shy, introverted person? Believe it or not, these are difficult questions because people get into big wars over such issues. If a person is only happy for herself, then she is limited to a little happiness; but when she is happy for other people, there is a lot more happiness. Thank God!

In Psalms 103:14, the Bible says, *"For he knoweth our frame; he remembereth that we are dust."* Brother Hyles often said that it was foolish for one dust ball to criticize another dust ball. Far too often, jealousy grips the heart of every person. How can you fight that attitude? What can you do but just say, "Oh, she is just jealous of me"? James 1:17 says, *"Every good gift and every perfect gift is from above, and cometh down from the Father of lights, with whom is no variableness, neither shadow of turning."*

There are some things you can do:

1. Take inventory in order to see what you have been given by God that the person next to you has trouble accepting in you and does not have.

2. Accept work at your own tolerance level and instead of having your preference level. Praise those who want to help at a project at which you are more professional and more experienced. You may know how to do it, and want to do it by yourself. That is why a lot of girls never learn anything in the home.

3. **Tell stories that specifically show exactly how you have struggled in the past.**

4. **Do not talk about your awards, projects, promotions, and honors.** Proverbs 27:2 says, *"Let another man praise thee, and not thine own mouth; a stranger, and not thine own lips."* Your work may not be so resented if you would not tell each step or detail over and over again. You are enjoying your job or the church project so much that you want to tell about it. The people around you really do not want to hear about all of that. I'm sorry, but they just don't. They are not *into* it like you are. Also, you usually do not even ask about them and their situations, and they feel useless because you always talk about your victories.

Did you know that those family Christmas form letters cause others to cringe? After all, everyone in the family sending the form letter has had great success in every area while the recipient reading the letter has lost a job, is home doing nothing following surgery, and is gaining weight—which is no fun!

5. **If you are a soloist, participate in a lot of teamwork.** Mrs. Beverly Hyles sings beautiful solos. After the church services, she greets the visitors or often helps another with a special need or problem. Every person can do the same. If you can charm all the ladies of the church while keeping a Martha Stewart home, assembling a beautiful wardrobe, and singing poetically, then be sure to volunteer to clean a lot of restrooms. Be available for the work nights.

6. **Jump on the side of the person who might have appeared to be jealous of you.** The fact is more of us are jealous people ourselves than we care to admit. Who are you dividing? Jealousy divides. You cannot dismiss the situation by saying, "Oh, they are jealous of me." If you do care about that

person or if someone has had a big burden in life, say, "I've been praying for you." Psalms 77:3, *"I remembered God, and was troubled: I complained, and my spirit was overwhelmed. Selah."*

    I believe we all fight jealousy. The difference is the ones who heed the warnings. Jealousy will come, so we need to look ahead and prepare before it comes. I have seen red flags warning me of jealousy ahead. Whom are you dividing? Whom should you let go? Should you free a relative, a friend, a helper, or a work colleague? Who is it right now? Your friend now likes and enjoys the company of other people. Don't divide over that wonderful opportunity. Friends don't ignore friends; they free them from jealousy. Whom do you need to let go free?

    Last, but not least, remember when the red flag appears ahead of you, prepare to fight the jealousy that comes your way. Remember, at one time or another, every person gets jealous. We need to fight the divisive sin of jealousy.

CHAPTER TWO

May I Be First?

> "We spend our time envying people whom we wouldn't wish to be."
>
> –J. Rostand

SINCE THE BEGINNING of time, mankind has wanted to be first, better, and best. Some of this desire to be better and then best is not wrong. It has caused much good to be accomplished, and it has also caused us as individuals to feel a sense of achievement in a way that gives us a thrill and excitement above and beyond anything the so-called pleasures of the world have to offer.

Good, clean competition can motivate us to become our best selves. But, at this point, I am speaking of "teacher, teacher, can I be first, always and forever and for sure, before everyone else?" And for what possible reasons? None, except to be able to compare ourselves among ourselves which is not wise. We ought to follow II Corinthians 10:12c which says, *"but they measuring themselves by themselves, and comparing themselves among themselves, are not wise."*

The Foolishness of Comparison Causes Jealousy

The foolishness of comparison causes jealousy and *"...jealousy is cruel as the grave: the coals thereof are coals of fire, which hath a most vehement flame."* (Song of Solomon 8:6b) I have watched young people ruin their opportunities for a better life because of comparing themselves with others.

Girls will come to me as Dean of Women at Hyles-Anderson College saying, "I am going to quit because everyone else has better grades and more credits than I do, so why should I stay in college?" When I ask them what they are receiving from their bus routes, classes, church services, chapel sermons, dormitory life, devotions, and on and on, they sometimes say, "I've never learned so much in my life. I am a better person for all those things." But, because of comparison, they sometimes go on and leave with very little hope of a good future.

One girl, of whom I'm thinking, didn't compare her training, physical stamina, home background, educational background, years as a Christian, years in the Bible, financial status, personality, appearance, or opportunities for gaining experience with others with whom she was comparing her grades and credits. There was no way for her grades to reflect all that training.

There are girls who are doing a great job simply just to get into college, to learn to obey rules, to work for room and board, to learn to listen and apply chapel and church sermons, to learn the give and take of dormitory life, to care for their grooming and clothes, to win souls, to acquire a steady Bible-reading habit, and to finish a couple of courses. For others, that would be complete failure. A girl who has grown up with hours and hours of good training from parents, pastors, Sunday school teachers, and Christian school teachers would be able to do all the things the first girl is learning to do long before she entered college.

The Foolishness of Comparison Causes Us to Hurt Others

Being the mother of one boy and one girl, I do not recall having a great deal of trouble with comparing one child with another or fending off remarks of comparison. Now that I'm the grandmother of six—four boys and two girls—I find that I cannot handle anything but praise for them, and, even then, I don't want praise for one above another. I want each of them to be praised for their own unique personalities, obedience, abilities, and beauty or handsomeness. Okay, so I'm a typical grandmother. I can't even say, "I'm so sorry." I believe it is much easier to fall into the foolishness of comparison when there are more children closer in age to compare. It also is easier to fall into this foolishness when there are two or more of the same gender.

Oh, how hurtful. Why can't we just say, "Sally has pretty hair," rather than, "I believe Sally's hair is going to be much prettier than Susie's"?

Some parents, grandparents, church nursery workers, Christian school teachers, and Sunday school teachers waste half their time comparing height, weight, weaning, potty training, walking, teething, and talking until, if it were truly known, we would find children hurting much of the time. I always tell a mother who is crying over her child's not being potty trained at the same age as other children that I've never seen a student come to college not potty trained! Foolish, foolish, foolish! Come on! We're not in some kind of race. Let's relax and enjoy training right attitudes into the precious children we teach in Sunday school or have in nursery class instead of telling how one is the worst about interrupting or whatever it might be. That's why we're there! We are to catch wrong thinking and, through Bible lessons, help those sometimes unruly children get some perspective. They're not there for us to complain about but to teach. Never, never, never tell a child or a class that they are the worst you've ever had.

I watched a whole high school class of a friend close to me go down over being labeled like that. If they're the worst, let's roll up our sleeves, shut up, and get to work. We've got a job to do.

The Foolishness of Comparison Causes Us to Hurt Ourselves Needlessly

"Susie had the same operation I had, and she was back on her feet caring for her family in one week. She even took baked goods to her elderly neighbors." Well, great for Susie. If she could really do it and not be back in bed two weeks later or not be paying twenty years later, fine. If she wasn't bragging about it and was keeping an even disposition, wonderful! Let's be proud of her and commend her. That has nothing to do with you. You might have had the same operation, but you're not the same person with the same physical and psychological makeup. You might have gone into the operation more physically depleted. You'll never know that; therefore, you do not have all the facts before you in order to compare. Get your answers ready so that you won't feel you have to defend yourself for not matching up to someone else in the re-entry race.

We Can Hurt Those Standing Around Us by the Foolishness of Comparison

"You're the best Sunday school teacher my child has ever had." This sounds fine until you notice a little lady overhearing what you said who just happens to have been your child's Sunday school teacher last year. Why can't we just say, "Katie surely enjoys your Sunday school class. You are a good teacher."

Several times I've been around Mrs. Pat DeCoster as I've gone to Turner, Maine, for *Christian Womanhood Mini-Spectaculars*. Now, she and her husband are responsible for several buildings being built on our college campus where I work, but I can never remember feeling that I must be careful around her because she has more money (to say the least) than I do. They just haven't chosen to live a life that would make me or others have to compare our bank balances. She looks to me for certain things that makes me feel she thinks I'm every bit as worthy as she is. She is just Pat and seems completely oblivious to the money God has given them the ability and common sense to make and use for God. She's Pat who, yes, happens to have money. If you have more of anything than someone else, realize that particular talents, gifts, or abilities can be a blessing to others, or they can put a wall between you and others.

May I Be First?

 Mrs. Beverly Hyles has enough beauty, charm, grace, graciousness, character, and leadership for ten women, and yet, I feel very good around her. That's a miracle! She's tall and model-like. I'm tall. Period! She's soft-spoken, and yet, is no namby-pamby; I'm just no namby-pamby! She carries a lacy handkerchief for no reason. I wear a napkin at my neck because I spill. It's a great blessing for me to be around Beverly Hyles. She makes me feel as if I'm very important to her.

 Wouldn't it be foolish for me to hurt others who work around Pat and me at a Mini-Spectacular or Beverly Hyles and me at a church function on account of my being cool toward either of them because I've compared myself unfavorably with them? Can I be first? Yes, I can. I can be first in God's love for me. What else really matters?

PART FIVE

The Conclusion

OH, MY DREAM and my burden for the girls at Hyles-Anderson College is that they be different. It is my dream that every man who is married to a Hyles-Anderson College girl will have a jewel—one of God's precious gems. She might not be beautiful, and perhaps won't be smart. There may be things she is not, but if she loves her husband, if she dresses modestly, if she wins souls, if she does not have a critical spirit, if she doesn't have a gossiping tongue, if she doesn't run around all nervous, worried and depressed, that man has a JEWEL!

I don't know if it is possible or not because we've never seen it. We have never seen a whole group of women like this. Would it be possible at your church? If you are reading this, you are probably a leader in your church. It is going to be true for the women of your church only if **you** decide to pay the price!!

I assure you that you will pay a price!! You will be tired many times! "I like to" and "I want to" have no part in the life of this kind of woman. You will have to get these words out of your vocabulary. There are only three questions:

1. Is it right?
2. Will it be good for me?
3. Does God want me to do it?

If God wants you to do it, then your husband will want you to do it. This kind of woman will not get upset when she is not asked to do something. She is not going to get upset when she is told to do something and is not allowed to do it because plans are changed. She will be ready whenever God wants to use her.

What a blessing that will be to the man of God in the church! What a blessing that will be to a husband and children! You will set the example. You will start becoming conscious about whether or not it is gossip when you start talking. I still do not think we know sometimes when we have a critical spirit or when we are disobeying our husbands. I think we are so used to doing it; it is so much a part of us.

I go into some churches, and they say, "I am so glad you are talking about the five sins of Christian women, but you don't have to talk like this in our church. Our ladies are so sweet! They get along with each other so well."

"Good," I say, "I'm glad to hear that." However, if afterward I don't hear the little backbitings as I go around the women, it will be the first church ever! Sometimes I will be in the restroom and they will not know I am there, and I hear what they say. I hear their talk.

Even if you say, "These aren't my problems!" yes, they are! If you are saying that these are not your problems, ask God to show you that they are your problems! I ask you to be a different woman!

I ask you to reread this book prayerfully and carefully. This book is not for unsaved women! The unsaved woman needs to be nervous, worried, and depressed because she really has problems! She needs to have Christ in her life!

Victorious Living by Victorious Christian Thinking!

I have shared many ways for you to practice and have victorious living by victorious Christian thinking!

Some of you are going to write back and say what has happened to you, and I'm going to cry for youi. I hope I cry more for you than you cry for yourself, for I hope by now that you've learned how to suffer well. Do you remember this little ditty? "When in trouble, when in doubt, run in circles, scream and shout!" That is the normal reaction. Isn't that dumb? But that is exactly what we do.

Ladies, are you going to try to be different? If so, read,

read, read! Memorize, memorize, memorize! Practice, practice, practice! Replace that negative thought with a positive, Bible-taught thought!

"Rejoice in the Lord alway: and again I say, Rejoice!"
(Philippians 4:4)

PART SIX

Doses of Scripture

Index of "Scripture Doses"

Assurance / 187
Broken Heart / 190
Can't Be Used / 191
Children / 193
Confidence / 194
Control Smart Mouth / 196
Death / 198
Dress / 200
Dying to Self / 201
Famine / 203
Fear / 205
Fun / 206
Holiness / 208
Human Relationships / 209
Inspiration of the Scriptures / 210
Jealousy / 211
Joy and Victory / 212
Latter Days / 214
Love / 215
Mind and Thoughts / 216
Obedience / 218
Patience and Waiting / 219
Prayer / 223
Purity / 226
Rest / 227
Righteousness / 228
Sickness and Suffering / 228
Soul Winning / 230
Speech / 231
Steadfastness / 232
Submission / 234
The Tongue / 236
Trouble / 250

Marlene Evans was an uncommon student of the Bible. One of the axioms that marked her life and was coined by her was, "Have a dirty Bible." She needed new Bibles every few months because hers were marked so much the words of the verses were difficult to read! Then, too, they were already falling apart with pages missing. She loved to make new Bibles into "dirty" Bibles.

A by-product of that intensive Bible study was what she called her "doses" of Scripture. In her daily counseling, she took note of the areas in which people struggled and turned to her Bible. She found Scriptures to help, had references typed on 3 x 5 cards, and gave them to her counselees to memorize and post. Her doses-of-Scripture 3 x 5 cards became legendary at Hyles-Anderson College.

Section VI of this book has been devoted to sharing Marlene Evans' doses of Scripture.

ASSURANCE

John 1:12
"But as many as received him, to them gave he power to become the sons of God, even to them that believe on his name."

John 5:24
"Verily, verily, I say unto you, He that heareth my word, and believeth on him that sent me, hath everlasting life, and shall not come into condemnation; but is passed from death unto life."

John 6:39, 40
"And this is the Father's will which hath sent me, that of all which he hath given me I should lose nothing, but should raise it up

again at the last day. And this is the will of him that sent me, that every one which seeth the Son, and believeth on him, may have everlasting life: and I will raise him up at the last day."

John 10:10
"*The thief cometh not, but for to steal, and to kill, and to destroy: I am come that they might have life, and that they might have it more abundantly.*"

John 10:14
"*I am the good shepherd, and know my sheep, and am known of mine.*"

John 10:28, 29
"*And I give unto them eternal life; and they shall never perish, neither shall any man pluck them out of my hand. My Father, which gave them me, is greater than all; and no man is able to pluck them out of my Father's hand.*"

John 11:26
"*And whosoever liveth and believeth in me shall never die. Believest thou this?*"

Romans 8:16-18
"*The Spirit itself beareth witness with our spirit, that we are the children of God: And if children, then heirs; heirs of God, and joint-heirs with Christ; if so be that we suffer with him, that we may be also glorified together. For I reckon that the sufferings of this present time are not worthy to be compared with the glory which shall be revealed in us.*"

Romans 8:35-39
"*Who shall separate us from the love of Christ? shall tribulation, or distress, or persecution, or famine, or nakedness, or peril, or sword? As it is written, For thy sake we are killed all the day long;*

we are accounted as sheep for the slaughter. Nay, in all these things we are more than conquerors through him that loved us. For I am persuaded, that neither death, nor life, nor angels, nor principalities, nor powers, nor things present, nor things to come, Nor height, nor depth, nor any other creature, shall be able to separate us from the love of God, which is in Christ Jesus our Lord."

Ephesians 1:13, 14

"In whom ye also trusted, after that ye heard the word of truth, the gospel of your salvation: in whom also after that ye believed, ye were sealed with that holy Spirit of promise, Which is the earnest of our inheritance until the redemption of the purchased possession, unto the praise of his glory."

Philippians 1:6

"Being confident of this very thing, that he which hath begun a good work in you will perform it until the day of Jesus Christ."

II Timothy 1:5

"When I call to remembrance the unfeigned faith that is in thee, which dwelt first in thy grandmother Lois, and thy mother Eunice; and I am persuaded that in thee also."

1 John 5:11-13

"And this is the record, that God hath given to us eternal life, and this life is in his Son. He that hath the Son hath life; and he that hath not the Son of God hath not life. These things have I written unto you that believe on the name of the Son of God; that ye may know that ye have eternal life, and that ye may believe on the name of the Son of God."

Jude 1:1

"Jude, the servant of Jesus Christ, and brother of James, to them that are sanctified by God the Father, and preserved in Jesus Christ, and called."

THE FIVE SINS OF CHRISTIAN WOMEN

BROKEN HEART

II Kings 8:11
"And he settled his countenance stedfastly, until he was ashamed: and the man of God wept."

Nehemiah 1:4
"And it came to pass, when I heard these words, that I sat down and wept, and mourned certain days, and fasted, and prayed before the God of heaven."

Nehemiah 8:9
"And Nehemiah…and Ezra the priest the scribe, and the Levites that taught the people, said unto all the people, This day is holy unto the LORD your God; mourn not, nor weep. For all the people wept, when they heard the words of the law."

Job 30:25
"Did not I weep for him that was in trouble? was not my soul grieved for the poor?"

Psalms 34:18
"The LORD is nigh unto them that are of a broken heart; and saveth such as be of a contrite spirit."

Psalms 30:5
"For his anger endureth but a moment; in his favour is life: weeping may endure for a night, but joy cometh in the morning."

Psalms 51:17
"The sacrifices of God are a broken spirit: a broken and a contrite heart, O God, thou wilt not despise."

Jeremiah 22:10
"Weep ye not for the dead, neither bemoan him: but weep sore for him that goeth away: for he shall return no more, nor see his native country."

Jeremiah 23:10
"For the land is full of adulterers; for because of swearing the land mourneth; the pleasant places of the wilderness are dried up, and their course is evil, and their force is not right."

Luke 6:21
"Blessed are ye that hunger now: for ye shall be filled. Blessed are ye that weep now: for ye shall laugh."

Luke 19:41, 42
"And when he was come near, he beheld the city, and wept over it, Saying, If thou hadst known, even thou, at least in this thy day, the things which belong unto thy peace! but now they are hid from thine eyes."

John 20:13
"And they say unto her, Woman, why weepest thou? She saith unto them, Because they have taken away my Lord, and I know not where they have laid him."

Philippians 3:18
"(For many walk, of whom I have told you often, and now tell you even weeping, that they are the enemies of the cross of Christ."

CAN'T BE USED

Isaiah 1:18
"Come now, and let us reason together, saith the LORD: though your sins be as scarlet, they shall be as white as snow; though they be red like crimson, they shall be as wool."

John 4:17-19
"The woman answered and said, I have no husband. Jesus said unto her, Thou hast well said, I have no husband: For thou hast had

five husbands; and he whom thou now hast is not thy husband: in that saidst thou truly. The woman saith unto him, Sir, I perceive that thou art a prophet."

I Corinthians 1:27

"But God hath chosen the foolish things of the world to confound the wise; and God hath chosen the weak things of the world to confound the things which are mighty."

I Corinthians 10:13

"There hath no temptation taken you but such as is common to man: but God is faithful, who will not suffer you to be tempted above that ye are able; but will with the temptation also make a way to escape, that ye may be able to bear it."

Philippians 3:13, 14

"Brethren, I count not myself to have apprehended: but this one thing I do, forgetting those things which are behind, and reaching forth unto those things which are before, I press toward the mark for the prize of the high calling of God in Christ Jesus."

I Timothy 1:12-15

"And I thank Christ Jesus our Lord, who hath enabled me, for that he counted me faithful, putting me into the ministry; Who was before a blasphemer, and a persecutor, and injurious: but I obtained mercy, because I did it ignorantly in unbelief. And the grace of our Lord was exceeding abundant with faith and love which is in Christ Jesus. This is a faithful saying, and worthy of all acceptation, that Christ Jesus came into the world to save sinners; of whom I am chief."

I John 1:9

"If we confess our sins, he is faithful and just to forgive us our sins, and to cleanse us from all unrighteousness."

I John 2:1, 2
"My little children, these things write I unto you, that ye sin not. And if any man sin, we have an advocate with the Father, Jesus Christ the righteous: And he is the propitiation for our sins: and not for ours only, but also for the sins of the whole world."
(See also Psalm 51.)

CHILDREN

Deuteronomy 6:6-9
"And these words, which I command thee this day, shall be in thine heart: And thou shalt teach them diligently unto thy children, and shalt talk of them when thou sittest in thine house, and when thou walkest by the way, and when thou liest down, and when thou risest up. And thou shalt bind them for a sign upon thine hand, and they shall be as frontlets between thine eyes. And thou shalt write them upon the posts of thy house, and on thy gates."

Deuteronomy 11:19
"And ye shall teach them your children, speaking of them when thou sittest in thine house, and when thou walkest by the way, when thou liest down, and when thou risest up."

Psalms 127:3
"Lo, children are an heritage of the LORD: and the fruit of the womb is his reward."

Proverbs 13:24
"He that spareth his rod hateth his son: but he that loveth him chasteneth him betimes."

Proverbs 19:18
"Chasten thy son while there is hope, and let not thy soul spare for his crying."

The Five Sins of Christian Women

Proverbs 22:6
"Train up a child in the way he should go: and when he is old, he will not depart from it."

Matthew 18:2, 3
"And Jesus called a little child unto him, and set him in the midst of them, And said, Verily I say unto you, Except ye be converted, and become as little children, ye shall not enter into the kingdom of heaven."

Luke 2:51, 52
"And he went down with them, and came to Nazareth, and was subject unto them: but his mother kept all these sayings in her heart. And Jesus increased in wisdom and stature, and in favour with God and man."

Ephesians 6:4
"And, ye fathers, provoke not your children to wrath: but bring them up in the nurture and admonition of the Lord."

CONFIDENCE

Psalms 27:1-3
"The LORD is my light and my salvation; whom shall I fear? The LORD is the strength of my life; of whom shall I be afraid? When the wicked, even mine enemies and my foes, came upon me to eat up my flesh, they stumbled and fell. Though an host should encamp against me, my heart shall not fear: though war should rise against me, in this will I be confident."

Psalms 65:5
"By terrible things in righteousness wilt thou answer us, O God of our salvation; who art the confidence of all the ends of the earth, and of them that are afar off upon the sea."

Psalms 118:8, 9

"It is better to trust in the LORD than to put confidence in man. It is better to trust in the LORD than to put confidence in princes."

Proverbs 14:26

"In the fear of the LORD is strong confidence: and his children shall have a place of refuge."

Isaiah 30:15

"For thus saith the Lord GOD, the Holy One of Israel; In returning and rest shall ye be saved; in quietness and in confidence shall be your strength: and ye would not."

Isaiah 41:10

"Fear thou not; for I am with thee: be not dismayed; for I am thy God: I will strengthen thee; yea, I will help thee; yea, I will uphold thee with the right hand of my righteousness."

Isaiah 54:17

"No weapon that is formed against thee shall prosper; and every tongue that shall rise against thee in judgment thou shalt condemn. This is the heritage of the servants of the LORD, and their righteousness is of me, saith the LORD."

Philippians 1:6

"Being confident of this very thing, that he which hath begun a good work in you will perform it until the day of Jesus Christ."

Philippians 3:4, 5

"Though I might also have confidence in the flesh. If any other man thinketh that he hath whereof he might trust in the flesh, I more: Circumcised the eighth day, of the stock of Israel, of the tribe of Benjamin, an Hebrew of the Hebrews; as touching the law, a Pharisee."

THE FIVE SINS OF CHRISTIAN WOMEN

II Timothy 1:7
"For God hath not given us the spirit of fear; but of power, and of love, and of a sound mind."

Hebrews 3:6, 14
"But Christ as a son over his own house; whose house are we, if we hold fast the confidence and the rejoicing of the hope firm unto the end. For we are made partakers of Christ, if we hold the beginning of our confidence stedfast unto the end."

I John 5:11-14
"And this is the record, that God hath given to us eternal life, and this life is in his Son. He that hath the Son hath life; and he that hath not the Son of God hath not life. These things have I written unto you that believe on the name of the Son of God; that ye may know that ye have eternal life, and that ye may believe on the name of the Son of God. And this is the confidence that we have in him, that, if we ask any thing according to his will, he heareth us."

CONTROL SMART MOUTH

I Samuel 2:3
"Talk no more so exceeding proudly; let not arrogancy come out of your mouth: for the LORD is a God of knowledge, and by him actions are weighed."

Job 8:2; 15:5-6; 16:10
"How long wilt thou speak these things? and how long shall the words of thy mouth be like a strong wind? For thy mouth uttereth thine iniquity, and thou choosest the tongue of the crafty. Thine own mouth condemneth thee, and not I: yea, thine own lips testify against thee. They have gaped upon me with their mouth; they have smitten me upon the cheek reproachfully; they have gathered themselves together against me."

Psalms 10:7

"His mouth is full of cursing and deceit and fraud: under his tongue is mischief and vanity."

Psalms 17:3, 10

"Thou has proved mine heart; thou hast visited me in the night; thou has tried me, and shalt find nothing; I am purposed that my mouth shall not transgress. They are inclosed in their own fat: with their mouth they speak proudly."

Psalms 38:13, 14

"But I, as a deaf man, heard not; and I was as a dumb man that openeth not his mouth. Thus I was as a man that heareth not, and in whose mouth are no reproofs."

Psalms 39:1, 9

"I said, I will take heed to my ways, that I sin not with my tongue: I will keep my mouth with a bridle, while the wicked is before me. I was dumb, I opened not my mouth; because thou didst it."

Psalms 141:3

"Set a watch, O LORD, before my mouth; keep the door of my lips."

Proverbs 15:1

"A soft answer turneth away wrath: but grievous words stir up anger."

Proverbs 18:19

"A brother offended is harder to be won than a strong city: and their contentions are like the bars of a castle."

Proverbs 25:28

"He that hath no rule over his own spirit is like a city that is broken down, and without walls."

The Five Sins of Christian Women

Proverbs 31:26
"She openeth her mouth with wisdom; and in her tongue is the law of kindness."

Ephesians 4:31
"Let all bitterness, and wrath, and anger, and clamour, and evil speaking, be put away from you, with all malice."

Colossians 4:5, 6
"Walk in wisdom toward them that are without, redeeming the time. Let your speech be alway with grace, seasoned with salt, that ye may know how ye ought to answer every man."

Hebrews 12:14
"Follow peace with all men, and holiness, without which no man shall see the Lord."

DEATH

Job 1:21
"And said, Naked came I out of my mother's womb, and naked shall I return thither: the LORD gave, and the LORD hath taken away; blessed be the name of the LORD."

Psalms 23
"The LORD is my shepherd; I shall not want. He maketh me to lie down in green pastures: he leadeth me beside the still waters. He restoreth my soul: he leadeth me in the paths of righteousness for his name's sake. Yea, though I walk through the valley of the shadow of death, I will fear no evil: for thou art with me; thy rod and thy staff they comfort me. Thou preparest a table before me in the presence of mine enemies: thou anointest my head with oil; my cup runneth over. Surely goodness and mercy shall follow me all the days of my life: and I will dwell in the house of the LORD for ever."

Psalms 116:15
"Precious in the sight of the LORD is the death of his saints."

John 11:25, 26
"Jesus said unto her, I am the resurrection, and the life: he that believeth in me, though he were dead, yet shall he live: And whosoever liveth and believeth in me shall never die. Believest thou this?"

John 14:1-7
"Let not your heart be troubled: ye believe in God, believe also in me. In my Father's house are many mansions: if it were not so, I would have told you. I go to prepare a place for you. And if I go and prepare a place for you, I will come again, and receive you unto myself, that where I am, there ye may be also. And whither I go ye know, and the way ye know. Thomas saith unto him, Lord, we know not whither thou goest; and how can we know the way? Jesus saith unto him, I am the way, the truth, and the life: no man cometh unto the Father, but by me. If ye had known me, ye should have known my Father also: and from henceforth ye know him, and have seen him."

II Corinthians 5:8
"We are confident, I say, and willing rather to be absent from the body, and to be present with the Lord."

Philippians 1:20, 21
"According to my earnest expectation and my hope, that in nothing I shall be ashamed, but that with all boldness, as always, so now also Christ shall be magnified in my body, whether it be by life, or by death. For to me to live is Christ, and to die is gain."

Philippians 4:7
"And the peace of God, which passeth all understanding, shall keep your hearts and minds through Christ Jesus."

The Five Sins of Christian Women

I Thessalonians 4:13-17

"But I would not have you to be ignorant, brethren, concerning them which are asleep, that ye sorrow not, even as others which have no hope. For if we believe that Jesus died and rose again, even so them also which sleep in Jesus will God bring with him. For this we say unto you by the word of the Lord, that we which are alive and remain unto the coming of the Lord shall not prevent them which are asleep. For the Lord himself shall descend from heaven with a shout, with the voice of the archangel, and with the trump of God: and the dead in Christ shall rise first: Then we which are alive and remain shall be caught up together with them in the clouds, to meet the Lord in the air: and so shall we ever be with the Lord. Wherefore comfort one another with these words."

I Peter 5:7

"Casting all your care upon him; for he careth for you."

Revelation 14:13

"And I heard a voice from heaven saying unto me, Write, Blessed are the dead which die in the Lord from henceforth: Yea, saith the Spirit, that they may rest from their labours; and their works do follow them."

Revelation 21:4

"And God shall wipe away all tears from their eyes; and there shall be no more death, neither sorrow, nor crying, neither shall there be any more pain: for the former things are passed away."

(See also I Corinthians 15:12-26; I Corinthians 15:51-58.)

DRESS

Deuteronomy 22:5

"The woman shall not wear that which pertaineth unto a man, neither shall a man put on a woman's garment: for all that do so are abomination unto the LORD thy God."

Proverbs 31:21, 22, 25, 30

"She is not afraid of the snow for her household: for all her household are clothed with scarlet. She maketh herself coverings of tapestry; her clothing is silk and purple. Strength and honour are her clothing; and she shall rejoice in time to come. Favour is deceitful, and beauty is vain: but a woman that feareth the LORD, she shall be praised."

Isaiah 47:2, 3

"Take the millstones, and grind meal: uncover thy locks, make bare the leg, uncover the thigh, pass over the rivers. Thy nakedness shall be uncovered, yea, thy shame shall be seen: I will take vengeance, and I will not meet thee as a man."

I Timothy 2:9, 10

"In like manner also, that women adorn themselves in modest apparel, with shamefacedness and sobriety; not with broided hair, or gold, or pearls, or costly array; But (which becometh women professing godliness) with good works."

I Peter 3:3, 4

"Whose adorning let it not be that outward adorning of plaiting the hair, and of wearing of gold, or of putting on of apparel; But let it be the hidden man of the heart, in that which is not corruptible, even the ornament of a meek and quiet spirit, which is in the sight of God of great price."

DYING TO SELF

Matthew 6:33

"But seek ye first the kingdom of God, and his righteousness; and all these things shall be added unto you."

Matthew 10:38, 39

"And he that taketh not his cross, and followeth after me, is not worthy of me. He that findeth his life shall lose it: and he that loseth his life for my sake shall find it."

Romans 6:11-13

"Likewise reckon ye also yourselves to be dead indeed unto sin, but alive unto God through Jesus Christ our Lord. Let not sin therefore reign in your mortal body, that ye should obey it in the lusts thereof. Neither yield ye your members as instruments of unrighteousness unto sin: but yield yourselves unto God, as those that are alive from the dead, and your members as instruments of righteousness unto God."

Romans 12:1, 2

"I beseech you therefore, brethren, by the mercies of God, that ye present your bodies a living sacrifice, holy, acceptable unto God, which is your reasonable service. And be not conformed to this world: but be ye transformed by the renewing of your mind, that ye may prove what is that good, and acceptable, and perfect, will of God."

I Corinthians 9:27

"But I keep under my body, and bring it into subjection: lest that by any means, when I have preached to others, I myself should be a castaway."

Galatians 2:20

"I am crucified with Christ: nevertheless I live; yet not I, but Christ liveth in me: and the life which I now live in the flesh I live by the faith of the Son of God, who loved me, and gave himself for me."

Philippians 1:21

"For to me to live is Christ, and to die is gain."

Colossians 3:2-3

"Set your affection on things above, not on things on the earth. For ye are dead, and your life is hid with Christ in God."

I Thessalonians 5:22
"Abstain from all appearance of evil."

II Timothy 2:3, 4
"Thou therefore endure hardness, as a good soldier of Jesus Christ. No man that warreth entangleth himself with the affairs of this life; that he may please him who hath chosen him to be a soldier."

II Timothy 2:11, 12
"It is a faithful saying: For if we be dead with him, we shall also live with him: If we suffer, we shall also reign with him: if we deny him, he also will deny us."

I Peter 2:24
"Who his own self bare our sins in his own body on the tree, that we, being dead to sins, should live unto righteousness: by whose stripes ye were healed."

(See also Psalm 101.)

FAMINE

I Kings 8:37-40
"If there be in the land famine, if there be pestilence, blasting, mildew, locust, or if there be caterpiller; if their enemy besiege them in the land of their cities; whatsoever plague, whatsoever sickness there be; What prayer and supplication soever be made by any man, or by all thy people Israel, which shall know every man the plague of his own heart, and spread forth his hands toward this house: Then hear thou in heaven thy dwelling place, and forgive, and do, and give to every man according to his ways, whose heart thou knowest; (for thou, even thou only, knowest the hearts of all the children of men;) That they may fear thee all the days that they live in the land which thou gavest unto our fathers."

The Five Sins of Christian Women

II Chronicles 20:9

"If, when evil cometh upon us, as the sword, judgment, or pestilence, or famine, we stand before this house, and in thy presence, (for thy name is in this house,) and cry unto thee in our affliction, then thou wilt hear and help."

Psalms 33:19

"To deliver their soul from death, and to keep them alive in famine."

Psalms 37:19, 25

"They shall not be ashamed in the evil time: and in the days of famine they shall be satisfied. I have been young, and now am old; yet have I not seen the righteous forsaken, nor his seed begging bread."

Matthew 6:25, 26

"Therefore I say unto you, Take no thought for your life, what ye shall eat, or what ye shall drink; nor yet for your body, what ye shall put on. Is not the life more than meat, and the body than raiment? Behold the fowls of the air: for they sow not, neither do they reap, nor gather into barns; yet your heavenly Father feedeth them. Are ye not much better than they?"

Matthew 24:7

"For nation shall rise against nation, and kingdom against kingdom: and there shall be famines, and pestilences, and earthquakes, in divers places."

Romans 8:35

"Who shall separate us from the love of Christ? shall tribulation, or distress, or persecution, or famine, or nakedness, or peril, or sword?"

Philippians 4:19

"But my God shall supply all your need according to his riches in glory by Christ Jesus."

FEAR

Joshua 1:9
"Have not I commanded thee? Be strong and of a good courage; be not afraid, neither be thou dismayed: for the LORD thy God is with thee whithersoever thou goest."

II Chronicles 20:15b
"Be not afraid nor dismayed by reason of this great multitude; for the battle is not your's, but God's."

Psalms 23:4
"Yea, though I walk through the valley of the shadow of death, I will fear no evil: for thou art with me; thy rod and thy staff they comfort me."

Psalms 37:25
"I have been young, and now am old; yet have I not seen the righteous forsaken, nor his seed begging bread."

Psalms 46:2
"Therefore will not we fear, though the earth be removed, and though the mountains be carried into the midst of the sea."

Psalms 56:3, 4
"What time I am afraid, I will trust in thee. In God I will praise his word, in God I have put my trust; I will not fear what flesh can do unto me."

Psalms 119:165
"Great peace have they which love thy law: and nothing shall offend them."

Proverbs 29:25
"The fear of man bringeth a snare: but whoso putteth his trust in the LORD shall be safe."

Isaiah 41:10

"Fear thou not; for I am with thee: be not dismayed; for I am thy God: I will strengthen thee; yea, I will help thee; yea, I will uphold thee with the right hand of my righteousness."

Isaiah 46:4

"And even to your old age I am he; and even to hoar hairs will I carry you: I have made, and I will bear; even I will carry, and will deliver you."

John 14:27

"Peace I leave with you, my peace I give unto you: not as the world giveth, give I unto you. Let not your heart be troubled, neither let it be afraid."

Philippians 4:11, 19

"Not that I speak in respect of want: for I have learned, in whatsoever state I am, therewith to be content. But my God shall supply all your need according to his riches in glory by Christ Jesus."

II Timothy 1:7

"For God hath not given us the spirit of fear; but of power, and of love, and of a sound mind."

I John 4:18

"There is no fear in love; but perfect love casteth out fear: because fear hath torment. He that feareth is not made perfect in love."

(See also Psalms 34:4-22.)

FUN

Exodus 15:2

"The LORD is my strength and song, and he is become my salvation: he is my God, and I will prepare him an habitation; my father's God, and I will exalt him."

Nehemiah 8:10
"...for the joy of the LORD is your strength."

Job 38:7
"When the morning stars sang together, and all the sons of God shouted for joy?"

Psalms 4:7
"Thou hast put gladness in my heart, more than in the time that their corn and their wine increased."

Psalms 35:9
"And my soul shall be joyful in the LORD: it shall rejoice in his salvation."

Psalms 100:2
"Serve the LORD with gladness: come before his presence with singing."

Psalms 126:2
"Then was our mouth filled with laughter, and our tongue with singing: then said they among the heathen, The LORD hath done great things for them."

Proverbs 15:13
"A merry heart maketh a cheerful countenance: but by sorrow of the heart the spirit is broken."

Proverbs 17:22
"A merry heart doeth good like a medicine: but a broken spirit drieth the bones."

Ecclesiastes 3:4
"A time to weep, and a time to laugh; a time to mourn, and a time to dance.

Ecclesiastes 8:15
"Then I commended mirth, because a man hath no better thing

under the sun, than to eat, and to drink, and to be merry: for that shall abide with him of his labour the days of his life, which God giveth him under the sun."

Habakkuk 3:18
"Yet I will rejoice in the LORD, *I will joy in the God of my salvation."*

Luke 6:21
"Blessed are ye that hunger now: for ye shall be filled. Blessed are ye that weep now: for ye shall laugh."

Philippians 4:4
"Rejoice in the Lord alway: and again I say, Rejoice."

I Thessalonians 5:16
"Rejoice evermore."

HOLINESS

II Corinthians 7:1
"Having therefore these promises, dearly beloved, let us cleanse ourselves from all filthiness of the flesh and spirit, perfecting holiness in the fear of God."

Ephesians 1:4
"According as he hath chosen us in him before the foundation of the world, that we should be holy and without blame before him in love."

Ephesians 4:24
"And that ye put on the new man, which after God is created in righteousness and true holiness."

I Thessalonians 4:7
"For God hath not called us unto uncleanness, but unto holiness."

I Peter 4:7
"But the end of all things is at hand: be ye therefore sober, and watch unto prayer."

HUMAN RELATIONSHIPS

Psalms 27:10
"When my father and my mother forsake me, then the LORD will take me up."

Psalms 39:3
"My heart was hot within me, while I was musing the fire burned: then spake I with my tongue."

Psalms 118:8
"It is better to trust in the LORD than to put confidence in man."

Romans 12:18
"If it be possible, as much as lieth in you, live peaceably with all men."

Romans 14:7
"For none of us liveth to himself, and no man dieth to himself."

Galatians 5:23
"Meekness, temperance: against such there is no law."

Galatians 6:2
"Bear ye one another's burdens, and so fulfil the law of Christ."

Ephesians 4:32
"And be ye kind one to another, tenderhearted, forgiving one another, even as God for Christ's sake hath forgiven you."

Philippians 2:4
"*Look not every man on his own things, but every man also on the things of others.*"

Philippians 2:14
"*Do all things without murmurings and disputings.*"

I Peter 2:17
"*Honour all men. Love the brotherhood. Fear God. Honour the king.*"

I Peter 3:8
"*Finally, be ye all of one mind, having compassion one of another, love as brethren, be pitiful, be courteous.*"

INSPIRATION OF THE SCRIPTURES

Joshua 1:8
"*This book of the law shall not depart out of thy mouth; but thou shalt meditate therein day and night, that thou mayest observe to do according to all that is written therein: for then thou shalt make thy way prosperous, and then thou shalt have good success.*"

II Timothy 3:16, 17
"*All scripture is given by inspiration of God, and is profitable for doctrine, for reproof, for correction, for instruction in righteousness: That the man of God may be perfect, throughly furnished unto all good works.*"

II Peter 1:21
"*For the prophecy came not in old time by the will of man: but holy men of God spake as they were moved by the Holy Ghost.*"

JEALOUSY

Genesis 37:4
"And when his brethren saw that their father loved him more than all his brethren, they hated him, and could not speak peaceably unto him."

Genesis 49:7
"Cursed be their anger, for it was fierce; and their wrath, for it was cruel: I will divide them in Jacob, and scatter them in Israel."

Job 5:2
"For wrath killeth the foolish man, and envy slayeth the silly one."

Proverbs 6:34
"For jealousy is the rage of a man: therefore he will not spare in the day of vengeance."

Proverbs 14:30
"A sound heart is the life of the flesh: but envy is the rottenness of the bones."

Song of Solomon 8:6
"Set me as a seal upon thine heart, as a seal upon thine arm: for love is strong as death; jealousy is cruel as the grave: the coals thereof are coals of fire, which hath a most vehement flame."

Romans 13:13
"Let us walk honestly, as in the day; not in rioting and drunkenness, not in chambering and wantonness, not in strife and envying."

James 3:14
"But if ye have bitter envying and strife in your hearts, glory not, and lie not against the truth."

The Five Sins of Christian Women

JOY AND VICTORY

Joshua 1:9
"Have not I commanded thee? Be strong and of a good courage; be not afraid, neither be thou dismayed: for the LORD thy God is with thee whithersoever thou goest."

Psalms 118:24
"This is the day which the LORD hath made; we will rejoice and be glad in it."

Proverbs 17:22
"A merry heart doeth good like a medicine: but a broken spirit drieth the bones."

Isaiah 59:19
"So shall they fear the name of the LORD from the west, and his glory from the rising of the sun. When the enemy shall come in like a flood, the Spirit of the LORD shall lift up a standard against him."

Nahum 1:7
"The LORD is good, a strong hold in the day of trouble; and he knoweth them that trust in him."

Habakkuk 3:17, 18
"Although the fig tree shall not blossom, neither shall fruit be in the vines; the labour of the olive shall fail, and the fields shall yield no meat; the flock shall be cut off from the fold, and there shall be no herd in the stalls: Yet I will rejoice in the LORD, I will joy in the God of my salvation."

John 10:10
"The thief cometh not, but for to steal, and to kill, and to destroy: I am come that they might have life, and that they might have it more abundantly."

John 16:22

"And ye now therefore have sorrow: but I will see you again, and your heart shall rejoice, and your joy no man taketh from you."

Romans 8:35-39

"Who shall separate us from the love of Christ? shall tribulation, or distress, or persecution, or famine, or nakedness, or peril, or sword? As it is written, For thy sake we are killed all the day long; we are accounted as sheep for the slaughter. Nay, in all these things we are more than conquerors through him that loved us. For I am persuaded, that neither death, nor life, nor angels, nor principalities, nor powers, nor things present, nor things to come, Nor height, nor depth, nor any other creature, shall be able to separate us from the love of God, which is in Christ Jesus our Lord."

I Corinthians 15:58

"Therefore, my beloved brethren, be ye stedfast, unmoveable, always abounding in the work of the Lord, forasmuch as ye know that your labour is not in vain in the Lord."

II Corinthians 2:14

"Now thanks be unto God, which always causeth us to triumph in Christ, and maketh manifest the savour of his knowledge by us in every place."

Ephesians 5:19, 20

"Speaking to yourselves in psalms and hymns and spiritual songs, singing and making melody in your heart to the Lord; Giving thanks always for all things unto God and the Father in the name of our Lord Jesus Christ."

Philippians 4:4

"Rejoice in the Lord alway: and again I say, Rejoice."

I Peter 1:8

"Whom having not seen, ye love; in whom, though now ye see him not, yet believing, ye rejoice with joy unspeakable and full of glory."

I John 5:4

"For whatsoever is born of God overcometh the world: and this is the victory that overcometh the world, even our faith."

LATTER DAYS

Isaiah 2:2

"And it shall come to pass in the last days, that the mountain of the LORD's house shall be established in the top of the mountains, and shall be exalted above the hills; and all nations shall flow unto it."

Micah 4:1

"But in the last days it shall come to pass, that the mountain of the house of the LORD shall be established in the top of the mountains, and it shall be exalted above the hills; and people shall flow unto it."

Acts 2:17

"And it shall come to pass in the last days, saith God, I will pour out of my Spirit upon all flesh: and your sons and your daughters shall prophesy, and your young men shall see visions, and your old men shall dream dreams."

I John 2:18

"Little children, it is the last time: and as ye have heard that antichrist shall come, even now are there many antichrists; whereby we know that it is the last time."

Revelation 9:6
"And in those days shall men seek death, and shall not find it; and shall desire to die, and death shall flee from them."

(See also II Timothy 3:1-7; II Peter 3:3-9.)

LOVE

Deuteronomy 6:5
"And thou shalt love the LORD thy God with all thine heart, and with all thy soul, and with all thy might."

Ruth 1:16
"And Ruth said, Intreat me not to leave thee, or to return from following after thee: for whither thou goest, I will go; and where thou lodgest, I will lodge: thy people shall be my people, and thy God my God."

Matthew 19:19
"Honour thy father and thy mother: and, Thou shalt love thy neighbour as thyself."

Matthew 22:39
"And the second is like unto it, Thou shalt love thy neighbour as thyself."

Mark 12:30
"And thou shalt love the Lord thy God with all thy heart, and with all thy soul, and with all thy mind, and with all thy strength: this is the first commandment."

Luke 10:27
"And he answering said, Thou shalt love the Lord thy God with all thy heart, and with all thy soul, and with all thy strength, and with all thy mind; and thy neighbour as thyself."

I Corinthians 13:4-6

"Charity suffereth long, and is kind; charity envieth not; charity vaunteth not itself, is not puffed up, Doth not behave itself unseemly, seeketh not her own, is not easily provoked, thinketh no evil; Rejoiceth not in iniquity, but rejoiceth in the truth."

Hebrews 4:16

"Let us therefore come boldly unto the throne of grace, that we may obtain mercy, and find grace to help in time of need."

I John 4:10, 19

"Herein is love, not that we loved God, but that he loved us, and sent his Son to be the propitiation for our sins. We love him, because he first loved us."

MIND AND THOUGHTS

Psalms 39:3

"My heart was hot within me, while I was musing the fire burned: then spake I with my tongue."

Proverbs 23:7

"For as he thinketh in his heart, so is he: Eat and drink, saith he to thee; but his heart is not with thee."

Romans 7:23

"But I see another law in my members, warring against the law of my mind, and bringing me into captivity to the law of sin which is in my members."

Romans 12:2

"And be not conformed to this world: but be ye transformed by the renewing of your mind, that ye may prove what is that good, and acceptable, and perfect, will of God."

II Corinthians 4:3, 4
"But if our gospel be hid, it is hid to them that are lost: In whom the god of this world hath blinded the minds of them which believe not, lest the light of the glorious gospel of Christ, who is the image of God, should shine unto them."

II Corinthians 10:4, 5
"(For the weapons of our warfare are not carnal, but mighty through God to the pulling down of strong holds) Casting down imaginations, and every high thing that exalteth itself against the knowledge of God, and bringing into captivity every thought to the obedience of Christ."

II Corinthians 11:3
"But I fear, lest by any means, as the serpent beguiled Eve through his subtilty, so your minds should be corrupted from the simplicity that is in Christ."

Ephesians 4:23
"And be renewed in the spirit of your mind."

Ephesians 6:12
"For we wrestle not against flesh and blood, but against principalities, against powers, against the rulers of the darkness of this world, against spiritual wickedness in high places."

Philippians 2:5
"Let this mind be in you, which was also in Christ Jesus."

James 4:8
"Draw nigh to God, and he will draw nigh to you. Cleanse your hands, ye sinners; and purify your hearts, ye double minded."

I Peter 5:8
"Be sober, be vigilant; because your adversary the devil, as a roaring lion, walketh about, seeking whom he may devour."

THE FIVE SINS OF CHRISTIAN WOMEN

OBEDIENCE

Acts 5:29
"Then Peter and the other apostles answered and said, We ought to obey God rather than men."

Romans 16:19
"For your obedience is come abroad unto all men. I am glad therefore on your behalf: but yet I would have you wise unto that which is good, and simple concerning evil."

II Corinthians 2:9
"For to this end also did I write, that I might know the proof of you, whether ye be obedient in all things."

Ephesians 6:1
"Children, obey your parents in the Lord: for this is right."

Colossians 3:20
"Children, obey your parents in all things: for this is well pleasing unto the Lord."

Hebrews 13:17
"Obey them that have the rule over you, and submit yourselves: for they watch for your souls, as they that must give account, that they may do it with joy, and not with grief: for that is unprofitable for you."

I Peter 1:2
"Elect according to the foreknowledge of God the Father, through sanctification of the Spirit, unto obedience and sprinkling of the blood of Jesus Christ: Grace unto you, and peace, be multiplied."

I Peter 1:14
"As obedient children, not fashioning yourselves according to the former lusts in your ignorance."

PATIENCE AND WAITING

Psalms 27:4
"One thing have I desired of the LORD, that will I seek after; that I may dwell in the house of the LORD all the days of my life, to behold the beauty of the LORD, and to enquire in his temple."

Psalms 37:7
"Rest in the LORD, and wait patiently for him: fret not thyself because of him who prospereth in his way, because of the man who bringeth wicked devices to pass."

Psalms 37:34
"Wait on the LORD, and keep his way, and he shall exalt thee to inherit the land: when the wicked are cut off, thou shalt see it."

Psalms 40:1
"I waited patiently for the LORD; and he inclined unto me, and heard my cry."

Psalms 46:10
"Be still, and know that I am God: I will be exalted among the heathen, I will be exalted in the earth."

Psalms 103:6
"The LORD executeth righteousness and judgment for all that are oppressed."

Psalms 107:9-14
"For he satisfieth the longing soul, and filleth the hungry soul with goodness. Such as sit in darkness and in the shadow of death, being bound in affliction and iron; Because they rebelled against the words of God, and contemned the counsel of the most High: Therefore he brought down their heart with labour; they fell down, and there was none to help. Then they cried unto the LORD in their trouble, and he saved them out of their distresses. He brought them

out of darkness and the shadow of death, and brake their bands in sunder."

Psalms 123:2

"Behold, as the eyes of servants look unto the hand of their masters, and as the eyes of a maiden unto the hand of her mistress; so our eyes wait upon the LORD our God, until that he have mercy upon us."

Proverbs 20:22

"Say not thou, I will recompense evil; but wait on the LORD, and he shall save thee."

Ecclesiastes 7:8, 9

"Better is the end of a thing than the beginning thereof: and the patient in spirit is better than the proud in spirit. Be not hasty in thy spirit to be angry: for anger resteth in the bosom of fools."

Isaiah 30:7

"For the Egyptians shall help in vain, and to no purpose: therefore have I cried concerning this, Their strength is to sit still."

Isaiah 30:15

"For thus saith the Lord GOD, the Holy One of Israel; In returning and rest shall ye be saved; in quietness and in confidence shall be your strength: and ye would not."

Isaiah 40:31

"But they that wait upon the LORD shall renew their strength; they shall mount up with wings as eagles; they shall run, and not be weary; and they shall walk, and not faint."

Lamentations 3:24, 25

"The LORD is my portion, saith my soul; therefore will I hope in him. The LORD is good unto them that wait for him, to the soul that seeketh him."

Lamentations 3:26
"It is good that a man should both hope and quietly wait for the salvation of the LORD."

Habakkuk 2:3
"For the vision is yet for an appointed time, but at the end it shall speak, and not lie: though it tarry, wait for it; because it will surely come, it will not tarry."

Zephaniah 3:8
"Therefore wait ye upon me, saith the LORD, until the day that I rise up to the prey: for my determination is to gather the nations, that I may assemble the kingdoms, to pour upon them mine indignation, even all my fierce anger: for all the earth shall be devoured with the fire of my jealousy."

Luke 21:19
"In your patience possess ye your souls."

Romans 5:3
"And not only so, but we glory in tribulations also: knowing that tribulation worketh patience."

Romans 8:25
"But if we hope for that we see not, then do we with patience wait for it."

Romans 12:12
"Rejoicing in hope; patient in tribulation; continuing instant in prayer."

Romans 15:4, 5
"For whatsoever things were written aforetime were written for our learning, that we through patience and comfort of the scriptures might have hope. Now the God of patience and consolation grant you to be likeminded one toward another according to Christ Jesus."

The Five Sins of Christian Women

I Corinthians 1:7
"So that ye come behind in no gift; waiting for the coming of our Lord Jesus Christ."

Galatians 5:22, 23
"But the fruit of the Spirit is love, joy, peace, longsuffering, gentleness, goodness, faith, Meekness, temperance: against such there is no law."

Colossians 1:11
"Strengthened with all might, according to his glorious power, unto all patience and longsuffering with joyfulness."

I Thessalonians 4:11
"And that ye study to be quiet, and to do your own business, and to work with your own hands, as we commanded you."

I Timothy 3:3
"Not given to wine, no striker, not greedy of filthy lucre; but patient, not a brawler, not covetous."

I Timothy 6:11
"But thou, O man of God, flee these things; and follow after righteousness, godliness, faith, love, patience, meekness."

II Timothy 2:24
"And the servant of the Lord must not strive; but be gentle unto all men, apt to teach, patient."

Hebrews 6:15
"And so, after he had patiently endured, he obtained the promise."

Hebrews 10:36
"For ye have need of patience, that, after ye have done the will of God, ye might receive the promise."

James 1:3, 4

"Knowing this, that the trying of your faith worketh patience. But let patience have her perfect work, that ye may be perfect and entire, wanting nothing."

James 5:7, 10, 11

"Be patient therefore, brethren, unto the coming of the Lord. Behold, the husbandman waiteth for the precious fruit of the earth, and hath long patience for it, until he receive the early and latter rain. Take, my brethren, the prophets, who have spoken in the name of the Lord, for an example of suffering affliction, and of patience. Behold, we count them happy which endure. Ye have heard of the patience of Job, and have seen the end of the Lord; that the Lord is very pitiful, and of tender mercy."

I Peter 2:20

"For what glory is it, if, when ye be buffeted for your faults, ye shall take it patiently? but if, when ye do well, and suffer for it, ye take it patiently, this is acceptable with God."

PRAYER

I Samuel 12:23

"Moreover as for me, God forbid that I should sin against the LORD in ceasing to pray for you: but I will teach you the good and the right way."

II Chronicles 7:14

"If my people, which are called by my name, shall humble themselves, and pray, and seek my face, and turn from their wicked ways; then will I hear from heaven, and will forgive their sin, and will heal their land."

Psalms 55:17

"Evening, and morning, and at noon, will I pray, and cry aloud: and he shall hear my voice."

Jeremiah 33:3

"Call unto me, and I will answer thee, and shew thee great and mighty things, which thou knowest not."

Matthew 6:5-8

"And when thou prayest, thou shalt not be as the hypocrites are: for they love to pray standing in the synagogues and in the corners of the streets, that they may be seen of men. Verily I say unto you, They have their reward. But thou, when thou prayest, enter into thy closet, and when thou hast shut thy door, pray to thy Father which is in secret; and thy Father which seeth in secret shall reward thee openly. But when ye pray, use not vain repetitions, as the heathen do: for they think that they shall be heard for their much speaking. Be not ye therefore like unto them: for your Father knoweth what things ye have need of, before ye ask him."

Matthew 7:7-11

"Ask, and it shall be given you; seek, and ye shall find; knock, and it shall be opened unto you: For every one that asketh receiveth; and he that seeketh findeth; and to him that knocketh it shall be opened. Or what man is there of you, whom if his son ask bread, will he give him a stone? Or if he ask a fish, will he give him a serpent? If ye then, being evil, know how to give good gifts unto your children, how much more shall your Father which is in heaven give good things to them that ask him?"

Matthew 9:38

"Pray ye therefore the Lord of the harvest, that he will send forth labourers into his harvest."

Matthew 17:21

"Howbeit this kind goeth not out but by prayer and fasting."

Matthew 18:19, 20

"Again I say unto you, That if two of you shall agree on earth as touching any thing that they shall ask, it shall be done for them of my Father which is in heaven. For where two or three are gathered together in my name, there am I in the midst of them."

Matthew 21:22
"And all things, whatsoever ye shall ask in prayer, believing, ye shall receive."

Matthew 26:40, 41
"And he cometh unto the disciples, and findeth them asleep, and saith unto Peter, What, could ye not watch with me one hour? Watch and pray, that ye enter not into temptation: the spirit indeed is willing, but the flesh is weak."

Mark 11:23, 24
"For verily I say unto you, That whosoever shall say unto this mountain, Be thou removed, and be thou cast into the sea; and shall not doubt in his heart, but shall believe that those things which he saith shall come to pass; he shall have whatsoever he saith. Therefore I say unto you, What things soever ye desire, when ye pray, believe that ye receive them, and ye shall have them."

Mark 11:25, 26
"And when ye stand praying, forgive, if ye have ought against any: that your Father also which is in heaven may forgive you your trespasses. But if ye do not forgive, neither will your Father which is in heaven forgive your trespasses."

Luke 6:12
"And it came to pass in those days, that he went out into a mountain to pray, and continued all night in prayer to God."

John 15:7, 16
"If ye abide in me, and my words abide in you, ye shall ask what ye will, and it shall be done unto you. Ye have not chosen me, but I have chosen you, and ordained you, that ye should go and bring forth fruit, and that your fruit should remain: that whatsoever ye shall ask of the Father in my name, he may give it you."

THE FIVE SINS OF CHRISTIAN WOMEN

Acts 12:5
"Peter therefore was kept in prison: but prayer was made without ceasing of the church unto God for him."

Romans 8:26, 27
"Likewise the Spirit also helpeth our infirmities: for we know not what we should pray for as we ought: but the Spirit itself maketh intercession for us with groanings which cannot be uttered. And he that searcheth the hearts knoweth what is the mind of the Spirit, because he maketh intercession for the saints according to the will of God."

Philippians 4:6
"Be careful for nothing; but in every thing by prayer and supplication with thanksgiving let your requests be made known unto God."

I Thessalonians 5:17
"Pray without ceasing."

(See also I Kings 18:41-45; Luke 18:1-8; James 5:13-18.)

PURITY

I Corinthians 6:19, 20
"What? know ye not that your body is the temple of the Holy Ghost which is in you, which ye have of God, and ye are not your own? For ye are bought with a price: therefore glorify God in your body, and in your spirit, which are God's."

Philippians 4:8
"Finally, brethren, whatsoever things are true, whatsoever things are honest, whatsoever things are just, whatsoever things are pure, whatsoever things are lovely, whatsoever things are of good report; if there be any virtue, and if there be any praise, think on these things."

I Timothy 4:12
"Let no man despise thy youth; but be thou an example of the believers, in word, in conversation, in charity, in spirit, in faith, in purity."

REST

Psalms 16:9
"Therefore my heart is glad, and my glory rejoiceth: my flesh also shall rest in hope."

Psalms 37:7
"Rest in the LORD, and wait patiently for him: fret not thyself because of him who prospereth in his way, because of the man who bringeth wicked devices to pass."

Isaiah 40:28-31
"Hast thou not known? hast thou not heard, that the everlasting God, the LORD, the Creator of the ends of the earth, fainteth not, neither is weary? there is no searching of his understanding. He giveth power to the faint; and to them that have no might he increaseth strength. Even the youths shall faint and be weary, and the young men shall utterly fall: But they that wait upon the LORD shall renew their strength; they shall mount up with wings as eagles; they shall run, and not be weary; and they shall walk, and not faint."

Mark 6:31
"And he said unto them, Come ye yourselves apart into a desert place, and rest a while: for there were many coming and going, and they had no leisure so much as to eat."

Acts 2:26
"Therefore did my heart rejoice, and my tongue was glad; moreover also my flesh shall rest in hope."

THE FIVE SINS OF CHRISTIAN WOMEN

Revelation 14:13

"And I heard a voice from heaven saying unto me, Write, Blessed are the dead which die in the Lord from henceforth: Yea, saith the Spirit, that they may rest from their labours; and their works do follow them."

RIGHTEOUSNESS

Matthew 5:6

"Blessed are they which do hunger and thirst after righteousness: for they shall be filled."

Philippians 1:11

"Being filled with the fruits of righteousness, which are by Jesus Christ, unto the glory and praise of God."

I Timothy 6:11

"But thou, O man of God, flee these things; and follow after righteousness, godliness, faith, love, patience, meekness."

II Timothy 3:15, 16

"And that from a child thou hast known the holy scriptures, which are able to make thee wise unto salvation through faith which is in Christ Jesus. All scripture is given by inspiration of God, and is profitable for doctrine, for reproof, for correction, for instruction in righteousness."

I John 2:29

"If ye know that he is righteous, ye know that every one that doeth righteousness is born of him."

SICKNESS AND SUFFERING

Psalms 41:3

"The LORD will strengthen him upon the bed of languishing: thou wilt make all his bed in his sickness."

Psalms 119:71

"It is good for me that I have been afflicted; that I might learn thy statutes."

John 9:3

"Jesus answered, Neither hath this man sinned, nor his parents: but that the works of God should be made manifest in him."

John 11:4

"When Jesus heard that, he said, This sickness is not unto death, but for the glory of God, that the Son of God might be glorified thereby."

Romans 8:16-18

"The Spirit itself beareth witness with our spirit, that we are the children of God: And if children, then heirs; heirs of God, and joint-heirs with Christ; if so be that we suffer with him, that we may be also glorified together. For I reckon that the sufferings of this present time are not worthy to be compared with the glory which shall be revealed in us."

II Corinthians 12:7-9

"And lest I should be exalted above measure through the abundance of the revelations, there was given to me a thorn in the flesh, the messenger of Satan to buffet me, lest I should be exalted above measure. For this thing I besought the Lord thrice, that it might depart from me. And he said unto me, My grace is sufficient for thee: for my strength is made perfect in weakness. Most gladly therefore will I rather glory in my infirmities, that the power of Christ may rest upon me."

Philippians 3:10

"That I may know him, and the power of his resurrection, and the fellowship of his sufferings, being made conformable unto his death."

Hebrews 5:8

"Though he were a Son, yet learned he obedience by the things which he suffered."

James 5:11

"Behold, we count them happy which endure. Ye have heard of the patience of Job, and have seen the end of the Lord; that the Lord is very pitiful, and of tender mercy."

I Peter 1:7

"That the trial of your faith, being much more precious than of gold that perisheth, though it be tried with fire, might be found unto praise and honour and glory at the appearing of Jesus Christ."

Revelations 21:4

"And God shall wipe away all tears from their eyes; and there shall be no more death, neither sorrow, nor crying, neither shall there be any more pain: for the former things are passed away."

SOUL WINNING

Proverbs 11:30

"The fruit of the righteous is a tree of life; and he that winneth souls is wise."

Matthew 28:19, 20

"Go ye therefore, and teach all nations, baptizing them in the name of the Father, and of the Son, and of the Holy Ghost: Teaching them to observe all things whatsoever I have commanded you: and, lo, I am with you alway, even unto the end of the world. Amen."

John 1:41, 42

"He first findeth his own brother Simon, and saith unto him, We have found the Messias, which is, being interpreted, the Christ.

And he brought him to Jesus. And when Jesus beheld him, he said, Thou art Simon the son of Jona: thou shalt be called Cephes, which is by interpretation, A stone."

Acts 1:8
"But ye shall receive power, after that the Holy Ghost is come upon you: and ye shall be witnesses unto me both in Jerusalem, and in all Judæa, and in Samaria, and unto the uttermost part of the earth."

Acts 5:42
"And daily in the temple, and in every house, they ceased not to teach and preach Jesus Christ."

James 5:20
"Let him know, that he which converteth the sinner from the error of his way shall save a soul from death, and shall hide a multitude of sins."

SPEECH

Psalms 19:14
"Let the words of my mouth, and the meditation of my heart, be acceptable in thy sight, O LORD, my strength, and my redeemer."

Proverbs 25:11
"A word fitly spoken is like apples of gold in pictures of silver."

Matthew 12:36
"But I say unto you, That every idle word that men shall speak, they shall give account thereof in the day of judgment."

Ephesians 4:29
"Let no corrupt communication proceed out of your mouth, but that which is good to the use of edifying, that it may minister grace unto the hearers."

THE FIVE SINS OF CHRISTIAN WOMEN

STEADFASTNESS

Isaiah 29:9

"Stay yourselves, and wonder; cry ye out, and cry: they are drunken, but not with wine; they stagger, but not with strong drink."

Isaiah 50:10

"Who is among you that feareth the LORD, that obeyeth the voice of his servant, that walketh in darkness, and hath no light? let him trust in the name of the LORD, and stay upon his God."

I Corinthians 15:58

"Therefore, my beloved brethren, be ye stedfast, unmoveable, always abounding in the work of the Lord, forasmuch as ye know that your labour is not in vain in the Lord."

I Corinthians 16:13

"Watch ye, stand fast in the faith, quit you like men, be strong."

Ephesians 6:10, 11

"Finally, my brethren, be strong in the Lord, and in the power of his might. Put on the whole armour of God, that ye may be able to stand against the wiles of the devil."

Philippians 4:4-8

"Rejoice in the Lord alway: and again I say, Rejoice. Let your moderation be known unto all men. The Lord is at hand. Be careful for nothing; but in every thing by prayer and supplication with thanksgiving let your requests be made known unto God. And the peace of God, which passeth all understanding, shall keep your hearts and minds through Christ Jesus. Finally, brethren, whatsoever things are true, whatsoever things are honest, whatsoever things are just, whatsoever things are pure, whatsoever things are lovely, whatsoever things are of good report; if there be any virtue, and if there be any praise, think on these things."

Philippians 4:13, 14
"I can do all things through Christ which strengtheneth me. Notwithstanding ye have well done, that ye did communicate with my affliction."

Colossians 2:5, 6
"For though I be absent in the flesh, yet am I with you in the spirit, joying and beholding your order, and the stedfastness of your faith in Christ. As ye have therefore received Christ Jesus the Lord, so walk ye in him."

I Thessalonians 5:16-24
"Rejoice evermore. Pray without ceasing. In every thing give thanks: for this is the will of God in Christ Jesus concerning you. Quench not the Spirit. Despise not prophesyings. Prove all things; hold fast that which is good. Abstain from all appearance of evil. And the very God of peace sanctify you wholly; and I pray God your whole spirit and soul and body be preserved blameless unto the coming of our Lord Jesus Christ. Faithful is he that calleth you, who also will do it."

Hebrews 3:14
"For we are made partakers of Christ, if we hold the beginning of our confidence stedfast unto the end."

Hebrews 6:19
"Which hope we have as an anchor of the soul, both sure and stedfast, and which entereth into that within the veil."

James 1:8
"A double minded man is unstable in all his ways."

I Peter 5:9
"Whom resist stedfast in the faith, knowing that the same afflictions are accomplished in your brethren that are in the world."

The Five Sins of Christian Women

II Peter 3:16-18

"As also in all his epistles, speaking in them of these things; in which are some things hard to be understood, which they that are unlearned and unstable wrest, as they do also the other scriptures, unto their own destruction. Ye therefore, beloved, seeing ye know these things before, beware lest ye also, being led away with the error of the wicked, fall from your own stedfastness. But grow in grace, and in the knowledge of our Lord and Saviour Jesus Christ. To him be glory both now and for ever. Amen."

SUBMISSION

Genesis 3:16

"Unto the woman he said, I will greatly multiply thy sorrow and thy conception; in sorrow thou shalt bring forth children; and thy desire shall be to thy husband, and he shall rule over thee."

Ephesians 5:22-24, 33

"Wives, submit yourselves unto your own husbands, as unto the Lord. For the husband is the head of the wife, even as Christ is the head of the church: and he is the saviour of the body. Therefore as the church is subject unto Christ, so let the wives be to their own husbands in every thing. Nevertheless let every one of you in particular so love his wife even as himself; and the wife see that she reverence her husband."

Colossians 3:18

"Wives, submit yourselves unto your own husbands, as it is fit in the Lord."

Titus 2:5

"To be discreet, chaste, keepers at home, good, obedient to their own husbands, that the word of God be not blasphemed."

I Peter 3:1, 5

"Likewise, ye wives, be in subjection to your own husbands; that, if any obey not the word, they also may without the word be won by the conversation of the wives; For after this manner in the old time the holy women also, who trusted in God, adorned themselves, being in subjection unto their own husbands."

God
II Chronicles 30:8
"Now be ye not stiffnecked, as your fathers were, but yield yourselves unto the LORD, and enter into his sanctuary, which he hath sanctified for ever: and serve the LORD your God, that the fierceness of his wrath may turn away from you."

I Peter 5:6
"Humble yourselves therefore under the mighty hand of God, that he may exalt you in due time."

Authorities
Romans 13:1-7—"Let every soul be subject unto the higher powers. For there is no power but of God: the powers that be are ordained of God. Whosoever therefore resisteth the power, resisteth the ordinance of God: and they that resist shall receive to themselves damnation. For rulers are not a terror to good works, but to the evil. Wilt thou then not be afraid of the power? do that which is good, and thou shalt have praise of the same: For he is the minister of God to thee for good. But if thou do that which is evil, be afraid; for he beareth not the sword in vain: for he is the minister of God, a revenger to execute wrath upon him that doeth evil. Wherefore ye must needs be subject, not only for wrath, but also for conscience sake. For this cause pay ye tribute also: for they are God's ministers, attending continually upon this very thing. Render therefore to all their dues: tribute to whom tribute is due; custom to whom custom; fear to whom fear; honour to whom honour."

Colossians 3:22
"Servants, obey in all things your masters according to the flesh; not with eyeservice, as menpleasers; but in singleness of heart, fearing God."

The Five Sins of Christian Women

Titus 3:1

"Put them in mind to be subject to principalities and powers, to obey magistrates, to be ready to every good work."

Hebrews 12:9

"Furthermore we have had fathers of our flesh which corrected us, and we gave them reverence: shall we not much rather be in subjection unto the Father of spirits, and live?"

Hebrews 13:7, 17

"Remember them which have the rule over you, who have spoken unto you the word of God: whose faith follow, considering the end of their conversation. Obey them that have the rule over you, and submit yourselves: for they watch for your souls, as they that must give account, that they may do it with joy, and not with grief: for that is unprofitable for you."

I Peter 2:13, 14, 18

"Submit yourselves to every ordinance of man for the Lord's sake: whether it be to the king, as supreme; Or unto governors, as unto them that are sent by him for the punishment of evildoers, and for the praise of them that do well. Servants, be subject to your masters with all fear; not only to the good and gentle, but also to the froward."

THE TONGUE

Job 27:4

"My lips shall not speak wickedness, nor my tongue utter deceit."

Job 33:3

"My words shall be of the uprightness of my heart: and my lips shall utter knowledge clearly."

Psalms 12:1-4

"Help, LORD; for the godly man ceaseth; for the faithful fail from among the children of men. They speak vanity every one with his neighbour: with flattering lips and with a double heart do they speak. The LORD shall cut off all flattering lips, and the tongue that speaketh proud things: Who have said, With our tongue will we prevail; our lips are our own: who is lord over us?"

Psalms 12:6

"The words of the LORD are pure words: as silver tried in a furnace of earth, purified seven times."

Psalms 15:1-3

"LORD, who shall abide in thy tabernacle? who shall dwell in thy holy hill? He that walketh uprightly, and worketh righteousness, and speaketh the truth in his heart. He that backbiteth not with his tongue, nor doeth evil to his neighbour, nor taketh up a reproach against his neighbour."

Psalms 31:18

"Let the lying lips be put to silence; which speak grievous things proudly and contemptuously against the righteous."

Psalms 34:13

"Keep thy tongue from evil, and thy lips from speaking guile."

Psalms 39:1, 3

"I said, I will take heed to my ways, that I sin not with my tongue: I will keep my mouth with a bridle, while the wicked is before me. My heart was hot within me, while I was musing the fire burned: then spake I with my tongue."

Psalms 50:19-21

"Thou givest thy mouth to evil, and thy tongue frameth deceit. Thou sittest and speakest against thy brother; thou slanderest thine own mother's son. These things hast thou done, and I kept silence;

thou thoughtest that I was altogether such an one as thyself: but I will reprove thee, and set them in order before thine eyes."

Psalms 51:15
"O LORD, open thou my lips; and my mouth shall shew forth thy praise."

Psalms 52:2-4
"Thy tongue deviseth mischiefs; like a sharp razor, working deceitfully. Thou lovest evil more than good; and lying rather than to speak righteousness. Selah. Thou lovest all devouring words, O thou deceitful tongue."

Psalms 55:21
"The words of his mouth were smoother than butter, but war was in his heart: his words were softer than oil, yet were they drawn swords."

Psalms 57:4
"My soul is among lions: and I lie even among them that are set on fire, even the sons of men, whose teeth are spears and arrows, and their tongue a sharp sword."

Psalms 59:7, 12
"Behold, they belch out with their mouth: swords are in their lips: for who, say they, doth hear? For the sin of their mouth and the words of their lips let them even be taken in their pride: and for cursing and lying which they speak."

Psalms 71:24
"My tongue also shall talk of thy righteousness all the day long: for they are confounded, for they are brought unto shame, that seek my hurt."

Psalms 106:33
"Because they provoked his spirit, so that he spake unadvisedly with his lips."

Psalms 119:171, 172

"My lips shall utter praise, when thou hast taught me thy statutes. My tongue shall speak of thy word: for all thy commandments are righteousness."

Psalms 120:2-4

"Deliver my soul, O LORD, from lying lips, and from a deceitful tongue. What shall be given unto thee? or what shall be done unto thee, thou false tongue? Sharp arrows of the mighty, with coals of juniper."

Psalms 139:4

"For there is not a word in my tongue, but, lo, O LORD, thou knowest it altogether."

Psalms 140:1-3

"Deliver me, O LORD, from the evil man: preserve me from the violent man; Which imagine mischiefs in their heart; continually are they gathered together for war. They have sharpened their tongues like a serpent; adders' poison is under their lips. Selah."

Psalms 140:9

"As for the head of those that compass me about, let the mischief of their own lips cover them."

Psalms 141:3

"Set a watch, O LORD, before my mouth; keep the door of my lips."

Proverbs 2:12

"To deliver thee from the way of the evil man, from the man that speaketh froward things."

Proverbs 4:24

"Put away from thee a froward mouth, and perverse lips put far from thee."

The Five Sins of Christian Women

Proverbs 5:2

"That thou mayest regard discretion, and that thy lips may keep knowledge."

Proverbs 5:3-5

"For the lips of a strange woman drop as an honeycomb, and her mouth is smoother than oil: But her end is bitter as wormwood, sharp as a twoedged sword. Her feet go down to death; her steps take hold on hell."

Proverbs 6:1, 2

"My son, if thou be surety for thy friend, if thou hast stricken thy hand with a stranger, Thou art snared with the words of thy mouth, thou art taken with the words of thy mouth."

Proverbs 6:12, 14

"A naughty person, a wicked man, walketh with a froward mouth. Frowardness is in his heart, he deviseth mischief continually; he soweth discord."

Proverbs 6:16-19

"These six things doth the LORD hate: yea, seven are an abomination unto him: A proud look, a lying tongue, and hands that shed innocent blood, An heart that deviseth wicked imaginations, feet that be swift in running to mischief, A false witness that speaketh lies, and he that soweth discord among brethren."

Proverbs 8:6-8

"Hear; for I will speak of excellent things; and the opening of my lips shall be right things. For my mouth shall speak truth; and wickedness is an abomination to my lips. All the words of my mouth are in righteousness; there is nothing froward or perverse in them."

Proverbs 8:13

"The fear of the LORD is to hate evil: pride, and arrogancy, and the evil way, and the froward mouth, do I hate."

Proverbs 10:8

"The wise in heart will receive commandments: but a prating fool shall fall."

Proverbs 10:10-14

"He that winketh with the eye causeth sorrow: but a prating fool shall fall. The mouth of a righteous man is a well of life: but violence covereth the mouth of the wicked. Hatred stirreth up strifes: but love covereth all sins. In the lips of him that hath understanding wisdom is found: but a rod is for the back of him that is void of understanding. Wise men lay up knowledge: but the mouth of the foolish is near destruction."

Proverbs 10:18-21

"He that hideth hatred with lying lips, and he that uttereth a slander, is a fool. In the multitude of words there wanteth not sin: but he that refraineth his lips is wise. The tongue of the just is as choice silver: the heart of the wicked is little worth. The lips of the righteous feed many: but fools die for want of wisdom."

Proverbs 10:31, 32

"The mouth of the just bringeth forth wisdom: but the froward tongue shall be cut out. The lips of the righteous know what is acceptable: but the mouth of the wicked speaketh frowardness."

Proverbs 11:9

"An hypocrite with his mouth destroyeth his neighbour: but through knowledge shall the just be delivered."

Proverbs 11:11-13

"By the blessing of the upright the city is exalted: but it is overthrown by the mouth of the wicked. He that is void of wisdom despiseth his neighbour: but a man of understanding holdeth his peace. A talebearer revealeth secrets: but he that is of a faithful spirit concealeth the matter."

The Five Sins of Christian Women

Proverbs 12:6

"The words of the wicked are to lie in wait for blood: but the mouth of the upright shall deliver them."

Proverbs 12:13, 14

"The wicked is snared by the transgression of his lips: but the just shall come out of trouble. A man shall be satisfied with good by the fruit of his mouth: and the recompence of a man's hands shall be rendered unto him."

Proverbs 12:17-20

"He that speaketh truth sheweth forth righteousness: but a false witness deceit. There is that speaketh like the piercings of a sword: but the tongue of the wise is health. The lip of truth shall be established for ever: but a lying tongue is but for a moment. Deceit is in the heart of them that imagine evil: but to the counsellers of peace is joy."

Proverbs 12:22

"Lying lips are abomination to the LORD: but they that deal truly are his delight."

Proverbs 13:2, 3, 5

"A man shall eat good by the fruit of his mouth: but the soul of the transgressors shall eat violence. He that keepeth his mouth keepeth his life: but he that openeth wide his lips shall have destruction. A righteous man hateth lying: but a wicked man is loathsome, and cometh to shame."

Proverbs 14:3

"In the mouth of the foolish is a rod of pride: but the lips of the wise shall preserve them."

Proverbs 14:5

"A faithful witness will not lie: but a false witness will utter lies."

Proverbs 14:7
"Go from the presence of a foolish man, when thou perceivest not in him the lips of knowledge."

Proverbs 14:23
"In all labour there is profit: but the talk of the lips tendeth only to penury."

Proverbs 14:25
"A true witness delivereth souls: but a deceitful witness speaketh lies."

Proverbs 15:2
"The tongue of the wise useth knowledge aright: but the mouth of fools poureth out foolishness."

Proverbs 15:4
"A wholesome tongue is a tree of life: but perverseness therein is a breach in the spirit."

Proverbs 15:7
"The lips of the wise disperse knowledge: but the heart of the foolish doeth not so."

Proverbs 15:23
"A man hath joy by the answer of his mouth: and a word spoken in due season, how good is it!"

Proverbs 15:26
"The thoughts of the wicked are an abomination to the LORD: but the words of the pure are pleasant words."

Proverbs 15:28
"The heart of the righteous studieth to answer: but the mouth of the wicked poureth out evil things."

The Five Sins of Christian Women

Proverbs 15:30
"The light of the eyes rejoiceth the heart: and a good report maketh the bones fat."

Proverbs 16:1
"The preparations of the heart in man, and the answer of the tongue, is from the LORD."

Proverbs 16:10
"A divine sentence is in the lips of the king: his mouth transgresseth not in judgment."

Proverbs 16:13
"Righteous lips are the delight of kings; and they love him that speaketh right."

Proverbs 16:21, 23, 24
"The wise in heart shall be called prudent: and the sweetness of the lips increaseth learning. The heart of the wise teacheth his mouth, and addeth learning to his lips. Pleasant words are as an honeycomb, sweet to the soul, and health to the bones."

Proverbs 16:27, 28, 30
"An ungodly man diggeth up evil: and in his lips there is as a burning fire. A froward man soweth strife: and a whisperer separateth chief friends. He shutteth his eyes to devise froward things: moving his lips he bringeth evil to pass."

Proverbs 17:4
"A wicked doer giveth heed to false lips; and a liar giveth ear to a naughty tongue."

Proverbs 17:7, 9
"Excellent speech becometh not a fool: much less do lying lips a prince. He that covereth a transgression seeketh love; but he that repeateth a matter separateth very friends."

Proverbs 17:20
"He that hath a froward heart findeth no good: and he that hath a perverse tongue falleth into mischief."

Proverbs 17:28
"Even a fool, when he holdeth his peace, is counted wise: and he that shutteth his lips is esteemed a man of understanding."

Proverbs 18:4
"The words of a man's mouth are as deep waters, and the wellspring of wisdom as a flowing brook."

Proverbs 18:6-8
"A fool's lips enter into contention, and his mouth calleth for strokes. A fool's mouth is his destruction, and his lips are the snare of his soul. The words of a talebearer are as wounds, and they go down into the innermost parts of the belly."

Proverbs 18:20, 21
"A man's belly shall be satisfied with the fruit of his mouth; and with the increase of his lips shall he be filled. Death and life are in the power of the tongue: and they that love it shall eat the fruit thereof."

Proverbs 19:1
"Better is the poor that walketh in his integrity, than he that is perverse in his lips, and is a fool."

Proverbs 19:5
"A false witness shall not be unpunished, and he that speaketh lies shall not escape."

Proverbs 19:9
"A false witness shall not be unpunished, and he that speaketh lies shall perish."

Proverbs 21:23
"Whoso keepeth his mouth and his tongue keepeth his soul from troubles."

The Five Sins of Christian Women

Proverbs 22:10, 11

"Cast out the scorner, and contention shall go out; yea, strife and reproach shall cease. He that loveth pureness of heart, for the grace of his lips the king shall be his friend."

Proverbs 22:21, 24, 25

"That I might make thee know the certainty of the words of truth; that thou mightest answer the words of truth to them that send unto thee? Make no friendship with an angry man; and with a furious man thou shalt not go: Lest thou learn his ways, and get a snare to thy soul."

Proverbs 23:16

"Yea, my reins shall rejoice, when thy lips speak right things."

Proverbs 24:1, 2

"Be not thou envious against evil men, neither desire to be with them. For their heart studieth destruction, and their lips talk of mischief."

Proverbs 24:17

"Rejoice not when thine enemy falleth, and let not thine heart be glad when he stumbleth."

Proverbs 24:28

"Be not a witness against thy neighbour without cause; and deceive not with thy lips."

Proverbs 25:8-11

"Go not forth hastily to strive, lest thou know not what to do in the end thereof, when thy neighbour hath put thee to shame. Debate thy cause with thy neighbour himself; and discover not a secret to another: Lest he that heareth it put thee to shame, and thine infamy turn not away. A word fitly spoken is like apples of gold in pictures of silver."

Proverbs 25:17-19

"Withdraw thy foot from thy neighbour's house; lest he be weary of thee, and so hate thee. A man that beareth false witness against his neighbour is a maul, and a sword, and a sharp arrow. Confidence in an unfaithful man in time of trouble is like a broken tooth, and a foot out of joint."

Proverbs 25:23

"The north wind driveth away rain: so doth an angry countenance a backbiting tongue."

Proverbs 26:20

"Where no wood is, there the fire goeth out: so where there is no talebearer, the strife ceaseth."

Proverbs 26:22-24

"The words of a talebearer are as wounds, and they go down into the innermost parts of the belly. Burning lips and a wicked heart are like a potsherd covered with silver dross. He that hateth dissembleth with his lips, and layeth up deceit within him."

Proverbs 26:28

"A lying tongue hateth those that are afflicted by it; and a flattering mouth worketh ruin."

Proverbs 29:20

"Seest thou a man that is hasty in his words? there is more hope of a fool than of him."

Proverbs 30:14

"There is a generation, whose teeth are as swords, and their jaw teeth as knives, to devour the poor from off the earth, and the needy from among men."

Ecclesiastes 10:11-14

"Surely the serpent will bite without enchantment; and a babbler is no better. The words of a wise man's mouth are gracious; but *the lips of a fool will swallow up himself. The beginning of the words of his mouth is foolishness: and the end of his talk is mischievous madness. A fool also is full of words: a man cannot tell what shall be; and what shall be after him, who can tell him?"*

Isaiah 54:17
"No weapon that is formed against thee shall prosper; and every tongue that shall rise against thee in judgment thou shalt condemn. This is the heritage of the servants of the LORD, *and their righteousness is of me, saith the* LORD.*"*

Isaiah 59:1-4
"Behold, the LORD's *hand is not shortened, that it cannot save; neither his ear heavy, that it cannot hear: But your iniquities have separated between you and your God, and your sins have hid his face from you, that he will not hear. For your hands are defiled with blood, and your fingers with iniquity; your lips have spoken lies, your tongue hath muttered perverseness. None calleth for justice, nor any pleadeth for truth: they trust in vanity, and speak lies; they conceive mischief, and bring forth iniquity."*

Isaiah 59:13
"In transgressing and lying against the LORD, *and departing away from our God, speaking oppression and revolt, conceiving and uttering from the heart words of falsehood."*

Malachi 2:6, 7
"The law of truth was in his mouth, and iniquity was not found in his lips: he walked with me in peace and equity, and did turn many away from iniquity. For the priest's lips should keep knowledge, and they should seek the law at his mouth: for he is the messenger of the LORD *of hosts."*

Romans 3:13, 14
"Their throat is an open sepulchre; with their tongues they have

used deceit; the poison of asps is under their lips: Whose mouth is full of cursing and bitterness."

Philippians 2:14
"Do all things without murmurings and disputings."

Colossians 3:8
"But now ye also put off all these; anger, wrath, malice, blasphemy, filthy communication out of your mouth."

I Timothy 3:8, 11
"Likewise must the deacons be grave, not doubletongued, not given to much wine, not greedy of filthy lucre; Even so must their wives be grave, not slanderers, sober, faithful in all things."

I Timothy 6:4, 5
"He is proud, knowing nothing, but doting about questions and strifes of words, whereof cometh envy, strife, railings, evil surmisings, Perverse disputings of men of corrupt minds, and destitute of the truth, supposing that gain is godliness: from such withdraw thyself."

Titus 1:10
"For there are many unruly and vain talkers and deceivers, specially they of the circumcision."

Hebrews 13:15
"By him therefore let us offer the sacrifice of praise to God continually, that is, the fruit of our lips giving thanks to his name."

James 1:26
"If any man among you seem to be religious, and bridleth not his tongue, but deceiveth his own heart, this man's religion is vain."

I Peter 3:8-11
"Finally, be ye all of one mind, having compassion one of another, love as brethren, be pitiful, be courteous: Not rendering

The Five Sins of Christian Women

evil for evil, or railing for railing: but contrariwise blessing; knowing that ye are thereunto called, that ye should inherit a blessing. For he that will love life, and see good days, let him refrain his tongue from evil, and his lips that they speak no guile: Let him eschew evil, and do good; let him seek peace, and ensue it."

III John 10

"Wherefore, if I come, I will remember his deeds which he doeth, prating against us with malicious words: and not content therewith, neither doth he himself receive the brethren, and forbiddeth them that would, and casteth them out of the church."

(See also Jeremiah 9:2-9; Jeremiah 18:18; Lamentations 3:61, 62; Ezekiel 36:3; James 3:5-18.)

TROUBLE

Psalms 32:8

"I will instruct thee and teach thee in the way which thou shalt go: I will guide thee with mine eye."

Psalms 34:6

"This poor man cried, and the Lord heard him, and saved him out of all his troubles."

Psalms 37:4, 5

"Delight thyself also in the Lord; and he shall give thee the desires of thine heart. Commit thy way unto the Lord; trust also in him; and he shall bring it to pass."

Isaiah 40:31

"But they that wait upon the Lord shall renew their strength; they shall mount up with wings as eagles; they shall run, and not be weary; and they shall walk, and not faint."

Matthew 11:28

"Come unto me, all ye that labour and are heavy laden, and I will give you rest."

Romans 5:3-5

"And not only so, but we glory in tribulations also: knowing that tribulation worketh patience; And patience, experience; and experience, hope: And hope maketh not ashamed; because the love of God is shed abroad in our hearts by the Holy Ghost which is given unto us."

Hebrews 11:35

"Women received their dead raised to life again: and others were tortured, not accepting deliverance; that they might obtain a better resurrection."

Hebrews 12:6

"For whom the Lord loveth he chasteneth, and scourgeth every son whom he receiveth."

Hebrews 13:5

"Let your conversation be without covetousness; and be content with such things as ye have: for he hath said, I will never leave thee, nor forsake thee."

James 5:11

"Behold, we count them happy which endure. Ye have heard of the patience of Job, and have seen the end of the Lord; that the Lord is very pitiful, and of tender mercy."

I Peter 1:4

"To an inheritance incorruptible, and undefiled, and that fadeth not away, reserved in heaven for you."

The Five Sins of Christian Women

WORK

Nehemiah 3:5
"And next unto them the Tekoites repaired; but their nobles put not their necks to the work of their Lord."

Nehemiah 4:6
"So built we the wall; and all the wall was joined together unto the half thereof: for the people had a mind to work."

Nehemiah 6:16
"And it came to pass, that when all our enemies heard thereof, and all the heathen that were about us saw these things, they were much cast down in their own eyes: for they perceived that this work was wrought of our God."

Job 1:10
"Hast not thou made an hedge about him, and about his house, and about all that he hath on every side? thou hast blessed the work of his hands, and his substance is increased in the land."

Proverbs 16:3
"Commit thy works unto the LORD, and thy thoughts shall be established."

Proverbs 31:31
"Give her of the fruit of her hands; and let her own works praise her in the gates."

Ecclesiastes 9:10
"Whatsoever thy hand findeth to do, do it with thy might; for there is no work, nor device, nor knowledge, nor wisdom, in the grave, whither thou goest."

Ecclesiastes 12:13, 14
"Let us hear the conclusion of the whole matter: Fear God, and keep his commandments: for this is the whole duty of man. For God

shall bring every work into judgment, with every secret thing, whether it be good, or whether it be evil."

Matthew 16:27
"For the Son of man shall come in the glory of his Father with his angels; and then he shall reward every man according to his works."

Matthew 23:5
"But all their works they do for to be seen of men: they make broad their phylacteries, and enlarge the borders of their garments."

John 9:4
"I must work the works of him that sent me, while it is day: the night cometh, when no man can work."

Acts 18:3
"And because he was of the same craft, he abode with them, and wrought: for by their occupation they were tentmakers."

I Corinthians 4:11, 12
"Even unto this present hour we both hunger, and thirst, and are naked, and are buffeted, and have no certain dwellingplace; And labour, working with our own hands: being reviled, we bless; being persecuted, we suffer it."

Ephesians 4:28
"Let him that stole steal no more: but rather let him labour, working with his hands the thing which is good, that he may have to give to him that needeth."

I Thessalonians 4:11, 12
"And that ye study to be quiet, and to do your own business, and to work with your own hands, as we commanded you; That ye may walk honestly toward them that are without, and that ye may have lack of nothing."

The Five Sins of Christian Women

II Thessalonians 3:8-12

"Neither did we eat any man's bread for nought; but wrought with labour and travail night and day, that we might not be chargeable to any of you: Not because we have not power, but to make ourselves an ensample unto you to follow us. For even when we were with you, this we commanded you, that if any would not work, neither should he eat. For we hear that there are some which walk among you disorderly, working not at all, but are busybodies. Now them that are such we command and exhort by our Lord Jesus Christ, that with quietness they work, and eat their own bread."

(See also Matthew 20:1-16.)

A Note from the Publishers

"The Speech Heard Around the World"

AS THE MUSKET shot heard in Lexington on April 19, 1775, was referred to as "the shot heard 'round the world," in the same figurative sense, the speech from which this manuscript is named has been heard around the fundamental Christian world.

That musket ball started a revolution that gave birth to this great land in which we live. This speech brought a revolution in thinking and living to women across America and gave birth to the *Christian Womanhood* newspaper as well as the Christian Womanhood Spectacular, an international ladies' conference. It also resulted in thousands of practical helps, tapes, and literally over a hundred books being published to help Christians.

Shortly after I was asked to become the managing editor of *Christian Womanhood*, I began to realize the magnitude of the ministry of Mrs. Marlene Evans. Though I had worked with her for 20 years in some of her ventures, I now had a view of her great work in total.

When I discovered that this massive ministry began after making one speech, I felt compelled to learn more about this one speech, "The Five Sins of Christian Women." (I am still confused as to how a list of twelve things can be called five sins—maybe it's a woman thing. She does explain how that works later though.) I felt that as a tribute to her and as a help to ladies across America, this speech and her teachings on the subject should be put into book form. So my staff set about working to make that happen, especially Mrs. Evans' long-time assistant editor, Mrs. Linda Stubblefield.

This speech is a classic; it will last for years, and so will the book in which it is contained. I believe we do a disservice to Mrs. Evans when we primarily remember her and pay tribute to her only as a long-time cancer survivor. (She lived over 18 years after being diagnosed with a killer cancer.) First and foremost, she was a Christian wife, a mother of two, a grandmother of six, a teacher, a psychologist, a great mind, and a happy person.

Christian Womanhood is pleased to publish this great speech—"this speech heard around the world." Let it revolutionize you!

–Dan Wolfe
Managing Editor